ADVANCE PRAISE

MW01026654

"The business world is recognizing .... importance of effective teams in getting projects done and keeping all organizations nimble and innovative. Which makes this book—based on a once-secret military memo written decades ago—so timely, and, indeed, urgent."

—Steve Forbes, Editor-in-Chief, *Forbes*

"An excellent primer for new managers, *The Memo* is also a great review for the experienced executive to revisit and improve his or her own leadership approach, and to identify opportunities to enhance organizational effectiveness. *The Memo* brings together, in an interesting way, the author's personal experience, with historical highlights of management, as developed and utilized by the U.S. military. With pertinent quotes from accomplished military and business leaders, Jack creates an excellent story about decision-making and organizational effectiveness. I am recommending *The Memo* to my son as the first book he should read as he takes on the challenges of his first managerial position."

—Lawrence J. Blanford, Retired President and CEO, Green Mountain Coffee Roasters, Inc.

"Want to know how to manage a large organization in a way that frees you to actually LEAD and empowers your people to develop into leaders who will become far more than you pay them? Jack Yoest has captured this simple, but seemingly elusive concept by borrowing the memo that won WW II. Your assignment is probably not THAT big, but if it won a world war, it is definitely worth your time!"

—Mike Huckabee, former governor of Arkansas, presidential candidate

"If you're a leader; a military general, a business executive, a football coach, or a new US president and were allowed one book to read, *The Memo* by John Yoest would be the one I recommend. The clarity of this superb book and the brilliance of the original

WW2 document, *Completed Staff Work*, is the roadmap to success in decision-making. The staff prepares the decisions; the decision maker makes the decisions. Sounds simple. *The Memo* makes it so."

–Ed Rollins, Former Reagan White House political advisor,
Reagan Bush Campaign manager, 1984,
Hall of Fame Political Consultant

"I wish Jack had written this years ago. This is a must-read for leaders of organizations and companies as well as smart employees who want to succeed. Time is the one thing we can't create more of, but this book helps us become more efficient and more effective—both as managers and as staffers."

–Susan B. Hirschmann, CEO, Williams & Jensen,
one of Washington, D.C.'s oldest independent lobbying firms.

"Whether you're a newbie or an old pro, be a better, wiser, more professional, and successful manager by learning from the geniuses who managed our victory in WWII using many Biblical principles. My friend Jack Yoest's book will empower you."

–Richard Viguerie, direct mail entrepreneur,
chairman of ConservativeHQ.com.

"If you are interested in being better as a leader or follower, then this is a must-read. *The Memo* will occupy a special spot on your bookshelf between *Message to Garcia* and *One Minute Manager Meets the Monkey*. It defeats the confusion and fears that consume people when they set out to lead people and manage projects. This was an extremely satisfying read because it breaks the mold of the stuffy academic language and tone usually found in such works. This book will surely point you in the right direction on how to win your own leadership/management battles."

–James M. Kimbrough IV, Lieutenant Colonel,
United States Army Chair, Military Science Department,
Professor of Military Science, The College of William and Mary
& Christopher Newport University

The
Memo

How the Classified Military
Document That Helped the
US Win WWII Can Help You
Succeed in Business

JOHN WESLEY YOEST, JR.

Post Hill
PRESS

A POST HILL PRESS BOOK
ISBN: 978-1-68261-395-5
ISBN (eBook): 978-1-68261-396-2

Post Hill Press
New York • Nashville
posthillpress.com

Published in the United States of America

For Charmaine,
wife, mother, CEO

TABLE OF CONTENTS

PART ONE
PURPOSE: WHAT IS *COMPLETED STAFF WORK?*

PART TWO
PROBLEM: WHY IS THERE A NEED FOR *COMPLETED STAFF WORK?*

ACKNOWLEDGEMENTS

WIFE CHARMAINE HAS READ AND re-read every word and made every page better. Every writer needs a spouse who buys bytes by the barrel. We often argued over troubled paragraphs and my incomplete shorthand. I am an introvert, and Charmaine says it seeps into my truncated vignettes. "Use words," she says. Helpful, that wordsmith-wife. But I apologized after losing the written altercations. (I lose all of them.) I married "way over my head." She gets the dedication.

I thought the memo on *Completed Staff Work* was an urban legend. I first learned of the document on the internet, so I knew it had to be true… But my teaching assistant at Catholic U, Christine Burias, ran down the original article in the *Army and Navy Journal.* It was real. Who knew? If Radar O'Reilly, from the hit TV comedy *M*A*S*H* is the countenance of *Completed Staff Work* in the Army, then Christine is it for academia. She always anticipated what was needed and then took action and got things done right. I was usually clueless but got the credit anyway. Management is like that.

The Alert Reader knows that Your Business Professor has the best five children on the planet—the Penta Posse. "Doesn't make sense" was the common refrain when they read passages. I get the same input from my students. But I do make corrections. I can sense patterns, even without a 360 evaluation. Their experiences appear in a few case studies, proving that all of life is high school. Thank you Hannah, John, Helena, Sarah and James, you each have more courage than I can imagine.

I am the luckiest guy in the academy. I was awarded a generous grant from the Dean's Fund in The Busch School of Business and Economics to underwrite *The Memo*. (Don't tell the committee, but I would have done it for free. Ain't America great, or what...?) The Dean at the time, Andrew Abela, is now Provost at The Catholic University of America. I take credit for that too.

The leadership of The Busch School of Business and Economics at CUA, Bill Bowman, Brian England, and Reza Saidi, were the best at management even if Your Business Professor was the worst at Followership. I got space and time and the courses I wanted to teach to flesh-out the teaching of *Completed Staff Work*.

I have been conducting human testing. Every one of my students for the past decade has been a human subject in the evaluation of the doctrine of *Completed Staff Work*. I would demand that they provide push-back (disguised as feedback) to tell me something I didn't know. Does the content make sense? Does it fit with the Natural Law of human emotion? Can the arts of leadership and followership be taught? Can a story convey the Commander's Intent? Faculty and students at The Catholic University of America and at the Northern Virginia Community College were quick to offer suggestions to make this a better product.

Faculty at CUA were also a source of free consulting. Max Torres is the Director of the Management Department and a winner of the Novak Award from the Acton Institute for the Study of Religion and Liberty. He instructs us that the job of the manager is to make decisions. Our work is to teach our students the science, and to get them to practice the art of managing. Max should see his emphasis, if not his words, in these pages.

Stew McHie runs the Masters of Science in Business Analysis at CUA. He is a seasoned manager in marketing from Exxon who reminds me that staff must know when the debating is over, the decision is made, and execution is to begin.

Bill Kirst, a former Navy officer who served in Vietnam and later at PricewaterhouseCoopers, knows how to get things done in large, complex organizations. He served as CFO to the Catholic archdiocese for the Military Services and offered guidance on obedience to regulation and exceptions to policy.

Kevin Forbes encouraged me to "volunteer" to present *The Memo* findings at CUA's annual University Research Day. Faculty, students, and the surrounding community came forth with vigorous debate. Nobody got hurt.

Harvey Seegers, also teaching at CUA, has advice to an aspiring chief of staff. He served in the Marine Corps as aide de camp to the Commandant of the U.S. Marine Corps Paul X. Kelley. The four-star general's directive was to, "never confuse your job with my job…" Seegers later served on the executive staff for Jack Welch. Seegers is a strategic expert in the balance of boss-deputy-staffer.

Andreas Widmer, a former Swiss Guard and past CEO of Dragon Systems Software, emphasizes that leaders must keep the core of a business narrow and focused. He makes the "cut" in executive—to concentrate business efforts in the same manner as entrepreneur Peter Thiel.

Some thirty years ago Charmaine and I were "parents" at the Intern House for the Leadership Institute headed by Morton Blackwell. The learning and the instruction is nonstop at this influential nonprofit. A number of vignettes in the book are rooted (and I might have even remembered to cite them) in his expertise that he so generously shares.

And, I have the best parents-in-law. Dr. Crouse (doctor Dad) and Dr. Crouse (doctor Mom) offered expert advice and support on *The Memo*. They removed the worst of the puns. The Crouses are both descended from a long line of Methodist missionaries. They only let me marry Charmaine because my name is John Wesley. Doctor Mom is the anchoress.

Little sister Helen has started a number of enterprises with an advanced degree in chemistry, like Jack Welch, I guess. She offered advice on repotting one's career every decade or so. Brother-in-law, David Philbrook is a serial entrepreneur who claims that most every new account his team creates is a matter of luck. And the harder his team works, as Thomas Jefferson would say, the luckier he gets.

David Crouse may, or may not, have ever driven recklessly across Kentucky, but he knows how to find friends. And I feel fortunate (or I have been blessed??) to be counted among them.

Few are more astute about the workings of political intrigue than Dan Gainor at the Media Research Center, in Your Nation's Capital. He has forever been a source of wisdom for my research and he has never sent me an invoice.

Colonel William Davis, the Executive Director of the General Douglas MacArthur Foundation in Norfolk, Virginia, was most helpful permitting backroom access to the Memorial. James Zobel, the MacArthur Memorial Archivist, was instrumental in providing the details and source for this management doctrine. I thought I would have to don spacesuit-like anti-contamination gear or at least wear latex gloves when handling *The* (original) *Memo* from General MacArthur's papers. But I must have appeared to be a trustworthy, clean, careful academic. Jim provided relevant and meticulous attention to detail in reviewing this historical document. If the practice of management is advanced in any way by *The Memo*, then he deserves credit.

Debby Englander at Post Hill Press gets the award for "Best Editor Ever." She made the word adjustments that made the difference that is between lightning and a lightning bug. (Apologies to Mark Twain.) I attempted to be a compliant, cooperative writer even as I lost documents and missed corrections and missed deadlines (see chapter 21). She was demanding and forgiving of Your (absent-minded) Business Professor. She was both at the same time. (How is that possible?)

Thank you to Billie Brownell, my managing editor at Post Hill Press. Billie did the heavy lifting on the manuscript originally weighted down with errors large and small. She earns the credit for the book cover. I consulted with a number of artists on the design and everyone loved it. I could not find a detractor even when everyone is supposed to be a critic. But not here. The president of Post Hill Press, Michael L. Wilson, has a team that anticipates (see chapter 1).

John Dolan-Heitlinger, CDR, USCGR(ret), graciously provided the source for another significant memo, *Completed Staff Work* by G. E. R. Smith, C. B. E., Brigadier General, DDST, Supply and Transport Branch, Admin HQ, First Canadian Army, 15 August 1943. John reminds us that this ally in WWII adopted the management doctrine in the European theater.

Frank Breeden was among the first to see an audience for this management doctrine. His advice was direct and rock solid. His recommendations were hard-hitting. His words were the sharpest of edged-weapons that cut deep but never left me bleeding. I still don't know how he did that. He made the work better. And he bought lunch.

Completed Staff Work is the demand for recommendations and for tolerance of experimentation and mistakes. Any errors here are mine.

INTRODUCTION

DID YOUR STAFF GET THE MEMO?

The driver stopped directly at the entrance to my office building. My assistant was there at the door. I am whisked to my office, settled into my Herman Miller Aeron chair (extra back support), coffee appears at my elbow (splash of cream, one packet brown sugar), and a red folder with decision documents helpfully tagged pointing to where I will sign-off with my signature.

I didn't read the documents. Why should I?

Eager, competent staff had studied the issues, developed options, vetted the alternatives, and made suggestions. These were recommendations that I could trust and endorse without a moment's hesitation. (I am a decisive kind of guy.) I would be done in an hour and looked forward to an early lunch meeting with our biggest customer—after I finished reading *The Wall Street Journal*.

I would have no trouble hitting my 2:10 tee time...

Okay, I was dreaming. Yes, I did enjoy each of the above points, and each did each occur to me over the last half-century. But they never happened all on the same day. Goodness, never in the same year. It is true that I teach this stuff, but it doesn't mean that I've ever experienced it first-hand without friction. But I can still dream. *A man's reach must exceed his grasp, or what's a heaven for?* and all that.

I was a very slow learner in the practice of corporate effectiveness and refused to benefit from the mistakes of others. And there wasn't much help for Actual People—especially in those atrocious Organizational Behavior seminars (yes, I've taught a few). But you,

Alert Reader, have in this slim volume the outline on Getting Work Done.

Every manager dreams of having an empowered, proficient team who will Anticipate, Adapt, and Learn! That type of team understands that the boss sets the organizational priorities and understands that the wish of the manager is the subordinate's command.

There is even an ancient Bible reference that offers a picture of getting things done with the active, thinking support of others. That's where the manager expects both obedience and initiative, and doing the right thing right.

> *When Jesus had entered Capernaum, a centurion came to him, asking for help. "Lord," he said, "my servant lies at home paralyzed and in terrible suffering." Jesus said to him, "I will go and heal him."*

Don't bother, says the soldier. Real leaders really don't work that hard:

> *The centurion replied, "…For I myself am a man under authority, with soldiers under me. I tell this one, 'Go,' and he goes, and that one, 'Come,' and he comes. I say to my servant, 'Do this,' and he does it." When Jesus heard this, he was astonished and said to those following him, "I tell you the truth, I have not found anyone in Israel with such great faith."* [1]

A Roman centurion would be in command of 100 men and support staff (servants). He was speaking of his authority and

---

1   This passage was written by Matthew in his eighth chapter of the Bible. He worked for the IRS; not a popular guy. As a tax collector for the Roman Empire we can imagine that he would have well understood the benefit of influence and the value of getting *Completed Staff Work* done in a very large organization.

more. It was the power to influence. It was the power of getting *Completed Staff Work*.

This is the heart of leadership and followership. It is remarkable, valuable, and rare. *Completed Staff Work* would have astonished even Jesus Christ.

This is supremacy that the Roman army could understand. The soldiers even had a word for it: *auctoritas*, which means "the power to get things done without lifting a hand."

Publisher and capitalist Steve Forbes describes this attribute and how the Emperor of the Roman Empire, Augustus, 63 BC to 14 AD, wielded his power:

> *In addition to his hold on government and the army, Augustus relied on an intangible aspect of power to get his way, something the Romans called auctoritas...*
>
> *...the word connotes the respect that a Roman male was shown by his fellow citizens in daily life because of his accomplishments, lineage, financial status, marriage, military service, the way he carried himself, and the people he associated with.*
>
> *A Roman who had auctoritas could get things done without ever having to give a direct order, and nothing meant more to him.*

We can envision this popular Emperor spending his days wandering deep in thought.

Is this Management by Walking Around? Maybe. But this works best on the "control" part of management, following the "plan, organize, and lead."

Walking-Around-Management puts all the work in a boss's inbox as casket-basket where tasks and dreams go to die.

However, Real Managers and Known-World Emperors just want the work done. And the team wants it done before the boss makes a nuisance of himself. The best teamwork is when a problem or opportunity is anticipated, researched, and addressed even before the boss gets back from his late lunch. The staff becomes all-knowing and acts on the manager's desire even before he asks.

Now, this is omnipotent-like empowerment. Of both staff and management.

The modern boss may never get to the nirvana dream-state of Management by TelePathicCommunication™ but *The Memo*, based on *Completed Staff Work*, will be our workaround, interim solution.

This is a simple "how to" book both for managers and individual expert contributors. We will cover *Completed Staff Work* in two directions: up and down the organizational chart where, counterintuitively:

- The managers will learn leadership—in how to "follow" the team.
- The team will learn followership—in how to "lead" the boss.

This is often called "Managing Up" whereby a staffer stealthily manipulates his boss.

But, in fact, *Completed Staff Work* is open mutual manipulation where everyone wins.

This information is divided into four parts. First, we will define *The Memo* and *Completed Staff Work*.

Second, we will review the Problem and explain "why" *Completed Staff Work* is necessary and the value to the individual contributor, the manager, and the organization. This is a win-win-win strategy.

Third is the Path where we learn to manage *Completed Staff Work*. Here we discuss the tactics of managing the process of getting the background work done for a management decision.

And finally, we will explain the Presentation to managing your manager. This is the persuasion segment where we learn how to sell to the boss.

Completed Staff Work is where there is nothing to add. *It is finished.* And so we begin.

PART ONE:

Purpose: What Is Completed Staff Work?

CHAPTER 1

Anticipation: The one word that describes *Completed Staff Work.*

"FIND OUT WHAT'S ON THE boss's report card." Joe had a simple answer to my question.

I was having some trouble so I went to visit Good Ol' Joe, another manager on my level on the organizational chart. I wanted to see how he got things done. Maybe steal some ideas.

Let's call it "research" not "theft of intellectual property" because, well, Joe, you know, was no intellectual...

So I asked him how he did it. Ordinarily, people are slow to give secrets to a "competitor" whether the person is inside or outside an organization. But Good Ol' (Slow) Joe was an open book and maybe not the sharpest tool in the shed. But—

He was hitting his numbers.

I was not.

So we walked and talked up and down his business silo. Suddenly a hand grenade came rolling down the hall and some insignificant nobody staffer jumped out of his cubicle and jumped on the bomb, protecting Joe from the blast.

We didn't see it coming. But his staff did.

The dust settled and we turned a corner and bumped into Ethel, his junior sales assistant. She was smiling. "Acme Industries just re-ordered twenty-five cases of our premium widgets." Joe would hit his numbers. Again.

I pulled her aside. "How did that happen?" I asked.

"The Acme buyer tries to get his purchase orders in before the end of the quarter," she said. "This order was a little larger."

"Why would he do that for us?"

Ethel gives me a blank stare. "To help Joe…"

I stand perplexed as Ethel scurries off, and I hear Joe talking on his cell phone to Jonathan, a business reporter with *Widget Insider*. Jonathan, as everyone knows, is a jerk who couldn't get a real job so he makes a living in libel and slander. He wrote an article about my numbers from last year and that troubled product launch—but it wasn't my fault (you know how hard it is to get good people). I hate him.

But Joe and Jonathan are laughing over some inside joke about the Rotary Club potluck. Who's got time for that nonsense anyway?

We walk past those paperwork weasels in the purchasing department. One of the vermin sees Joe and rudely bellows to his superior, "Yo Joe, we just received your new monitors."

"Thanks," says Joe, "you're the best."

"No problem" the bootlicker replies. "But I'll need the DD 214 request and routing numbers by next month."

I stop. I've been trying for weeks to get those computer monitors. Every time I order something from those slackers, they say I need to completely fill out the forms with signatures and numbers in triplicate hard-copy with a six-week lead time. Sometimes I might leave a box or two empty but that's no reason to bounce the form back to me. And sometimes I wonder why I even bother since those dolts lose my paperwork half the time anyway.

"Joe," I ask, "does purchasing process your requests even before you do the paperwork?"

"Sure," he says. "Why do you ask?"

We walk into Joe's office and in walks Bob Big Boss. (This is odd; he has never been to my office.) Anyway I'm excited to corner him, "Bob, we need to talk; those people in purchase—"

"Later," Bob cuts me off and says to Joe, "I talked to the board and they approved the new budget and signed-off on your capital request."

I was ignored. And then I wondered where the board was going to get the additional money for Joe's project. Especially since I can't get anything done unless I get that 25 percent increase I demanded. This wasn't fair.

Bob smiles at Joe, and the Big Boss exits.

I ask Joe, "Budget? How did that all happen?"

Joe shrugs his shoulders, "Anticipation, I guess. I thought maybe the project would make Bob look good."

Lord almighty. What a simpleton. I had wasted a morning (and you know my staff was goofing off the whole time I was gone).

Ethel walks into Joe's office looking at her tablet as I make my leave. She was not interrupting much. I didn't see that he was doing much work anyway.

"Congratulations, Joe" I heard Ethel gush as I walked down the hall. "Great quote in the *Insider*... "

We all know that Joe. He's the Fair Haired Boss's Boy who doesn't do anything and gets everything handed to him.

And he hits his numbers.

And he is likeable.

I've always distrusted that Joe.

I'm working late. He always leaves at 5.

I'm working weekends. He's playing golf with the comptroller.

Nobody sees how hard I work and sweat (why is it always so hot in my office?) (What's with those idiots in maintenance)?

Nobody appreciates me.

Everybody loves Good Ol' Joe.

He hits his numbers.

The boss likes that.

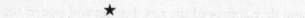

Years ago, Your Business Professor worked with some very talented managers Who Got Things Done. I was not one of them. I didn't understand *Completed Staff Work* and how it could change my life. I didn't know the secret of how Joe got the work done without breaking a sweat and always made his forecast, every single month.

Joe had trained his people to deliver *Completed Staff Work*. Or maybe his people had trained him—it could go either way. (Remember, Joe is really not that bright.) This policy begins with anticipation.

Here's what Joe and Joe's team was getting done: *The Staffer Works and The Manager Decides* where the objective is a finished recommendation.

Managers often complain that their direct reports are running out of work while the boss is running out of time. Some managers do this non-delegation, the amateurs like Your (younger) Business Professor.

But this is not always the fault of the individual contributor. Sometimes the manager does not know what direction or instructions to give his direct reports.

Managers know that their job is to Plan, Organize, Lead, and Control. And managers are working too hard. After all, they believe the myth that this is what that "lead" part of management is: to do everything.

It is true that the leading part might be the easiest for talented managers. But the boss cannot, must not, do all the thinking. This is why the best organizations have some form of *Completed Staff Work*. The staff does the hands-on labor and the manager makes decisions.

Here is what it looks like. A problem or opportunity is presented by the manager or uncovered by the staff. It doesn't matter how the assignment originates; the staffer using the *Completed Staff Work* method will follow this simple three-step outline:

1. Research the landscape, exploring for nearly all possible possibilities.
2. Develop a number of likely options, scenarios, and solutions.
3. Finalize and present (sell) a recommendation.

Note that the manager did little work in this phase. The work is done by the staff. It is complete. The boss can accept or reject or modify the recommendation. **Yes** or **No** or **Change**.

But usually the manager will simply adopt the staff recommendation. When *Completed Staff Work* is done the right way, the manager essentially makes a decision by just signing his name. This is why the "leading" can be simple.

Leadership is most critical when there is much more at risk than hitting a quarterly number. Human life can be at stake. The military understands this danger.

★

The origin of the phrase *"Completed Staff Work"* probably belongs to Archer L. Lerch, Major General, U.S.A., Provost Marshal General of the Army of the United States. Lerch, as a Colonel, wrote a memo to his staff, which was published in the January 24, 1942, edition of the *United States Army and Navy Journal and Gazette*. It was designed to pierce the haze and confusion in the fog of war.

U.S. General Douglas MacArthur also circulated the *Completed Staff Work* memo.

The military called it a doctrine because it is a belief system and a set of teachings. The word "doctrine" has religious connotations— as well it should. *Completed Staff Work* should be faithfully executed.

The policy was once labeled RESTRICTED in keeping with Army regulations. A document will be classified and marked "Restricted" when the information it contains is for official use only or of such nature that its disclosure should be limited for reasons of administrative privacy, or should be denied the general public.

This memo, this philosophy, won World War II.

Completed Staff Work was so vital to the war effort that it had its own security classification limiting its distribution to prevent it from falling into enemy hands. Fortunately, after the war, *Completed Staff Work* made it to the public domain. Following are portions from General Lerch's original memo, for your eyes only:

"Completed Staff Work" is the study of a problem, and presentation of a solution, by a staff officer, in such form that all that remains to be done on the part of the head of the staff division, or the commander, is to indicate his approval or disapproval of the completed action.

It is your duty as a staff officer to work out the details. You should not consult your chief in the determination of those details, no matter how perplexing they may be. You may and should consult other staff officers. The product, whether it involves the pronouncement of a new policy or affect an established one, should when presented to the chief for approval or disapproval, be worked out in finished form.

It is your job to advise your chief what he ought to do, not to ask him what you ought to do. He needs your answers, not questions. Your job is to study, write, restudy and rewrite until you have evolved a single proposed action—the best one of all you have considered. Your chief merely approves or disapproves.

In most instances, completed staff work results in a single document prepared for the signature of the chief, without accompanying comment.

The "completed staff work" theory may result in more work for the staff officer, but it results in more freedom for the chief. This is as it should be. Further, it accomplishes two things:

1. *The chief is protected from half-baked ideas, voluminous memoranda, and immature oral presentations.*
2. *The staff officer who has a real idea to sell is enabled more readily to find a market.*

When you have finished your "completed staff work" the final test is this: If you were the chief would you be willing to sign the paper you have prepared, and stake your professional reputation on its being right? If the answer is negative, take it back and work it over because it is not yet "completed staff work."

Business goals—as in war—are met when a team gets The Memo.

Anticipation describes *Completed Staff Work*. The best managers are never surprised. Avoiding the unexpected only happens with well-trained staffers who can identify opportunities and threats to the organization and then bring the warnings or good news to the attention of the boss.

★

Discussion Questions
1. How does the manager benefit when the staff anticipates?
2. How does the staffer benefit when the team anticipates?
3. How does the organization benefit when everyone anticipates?

CHAPTER 2

Decision: Putting the ˣcutˣ back into executive.

"ONE MUST BE A GOOD butcher," said William Gladstone, who served as Great Britain's Prime Minister in the late 1800s. A good CEO must be willing to make personnel cuts, cut a deal, cut out the nonsense, and cut to the heart of the matter.

Making a decision means picking an option and taking the other courses of action off the table. The boss separates the gold from the dross.

Scott Snook and Jeffrey T. Polzer wrote of this management challenge in a case study for Harvard Business School. (Snook 2004)

They use a coach's dilemma in *The Army Crew Team*. Under the heading, *The Elements of Success*, Snook and Polzer provide important insight into the importance of focus in decision-making using research from the U. S. Olympic Committee. A survey of dozens of rowing coaches, who were asked to rank the importance of over two hundred variables, found something surprising: less is more.

Interestingly, the importance assigned to [these] categories varied with the coaches' level of experience.

One pattern was that novice and intermediate coaches tended to rate a multitude of variables…as highly important…

…whereas master coaches focused on a smaller set of variables…

Amateur managers, like young coaches, are swamped with the number of inputs and variables that bombard them in the corner office. The novice manager does not know what to ignore so he ignores nothing and evaluates everything, which improves nothing.

The experienced coach/manager has the wisdom and judgment to determine what is important and what can be left out. Experience and practice produces a fine filter separating what is needed and valuable from what is less useful. This seasoning can take decades to produce a competent senior manager.

The staffer, as an individual contributor, is the one who "does the work"—sifts through the overwhelming barrage of data and options—so that the manager can make a focused decision.

Most of the manager's decision-making work will be deciding "what to do" and "what not to do." He will spend most of his management time cutting away and making a difference and decisions suitable to his pay-grade.

So the CEO must focus on only the moves that most leverage his time for greatest impact. How does he decide what those few things will be? Venture Capitalist and Chief Executive Officer trainer Fred Wilson recommends that, "A CEO does only three things."

1. Sets the overall vision and strategy of the company and communicates it to all stakeholders.
2. Recruits, hires, and retains the very best talent for the company.
3. Makes sure there is always enough cash in the bank.

The manager must understand these priorities and decide to decide. The best CEOs cut to the chase. The words "decide," "concise," and "scissors" share a root word—to cut away. Decide is a verb from the late fourteenth century, meaning "to settle a dispute," from the Old French *decider*, from the Latin *decidere* "to decide, determine"—literally—"to cut off."

The word "to decide" originates in *de-* "off" and *caedere* "to cut" and gives us resolution "at a stroke." The meaning, "to make up one's mind," was first used in 1830.

But the manager cannot do this alone. The bigger the decision, the more the need for a staffed-out recommendation that is reviewed and vetted by stakeholders. The decision-maker needs *Completed Staff Work*—from the options suggested by his team.

The boss decides.

What is the first step in becoming a decision-maker?

The desire to be a decider.

The Army Armor School was welcoming a new class. There were more than 60 of us new lieutenants in the section, and it seemed that no one wanted to be in charge.

Odd. Officers who didn't want to lead?

The instructors asked the class for candidates who would be willing to be interviewed for Class Leader. No extra credit; no rank; no compensation.

More work; no more money. (I didn't know it then but this is how most managers start.)

There were a few who stood up. I joined three classmates as the school faculty privately questioned us one-by-one. The lieutenants were quizzed. As the two others left, I could hear them muttering, "I don't know anything about classroom formations or emergency procedures or…"

They didn't know all the answers, and neither did I. But I stayed.

★

The most significant factor in establishing who is going to be a manager is that person's desire to be in charge. A person has to want the job. Even if others are in the position, the would-be manager will get off the bench and assert, "Put me in, coach."

Many people fear taking on the role of a manager because they're terrified of making instant, flawless decisions. Can they make decisions under time pressures when they're facing ambiguity and uncertainty and confusion?

General George Patton said, "A good plan, violently executed now, is better than a perfect plan next week." The manager needs to learn that he must step-up and step-in with a timely plan or *he* may be "violently executed." It is better to be "good enough" now than "perfect" later.

Remember: Even a poor plan, properly executed, is better than a proper plan, poorly executed.

Military wisdom is based on experience in life-and-death situations, and an awareness that circumstances and events constantly change. As the nineteenth century German Field Marshall Moltke (the elder) noted, a meticulously crafted operations plan does not survive contact with the enemy. A business plan often does not survive contact with a customer.

Even in a risky battlefield in the fog of war, the commanders keep moving, keep adjusting, and keep advancing. Stuff happens. Things change. Risk is inevitable.

A business manager screws up and he gets sacked. The military manager screws up and someone comes home in a sack. The stakes for the uniformed services include the "last full measure" of more than the bottom line. Even though the stakes are higher and the pressures greater, the need for decision-making is the same.

Everyone in the corporate world should understand that there are always hazards. The best bosses are decision-makers who use *Completed Staff Work*. The military is practiced in this doctrine because the stakes of losing are higher. Some might suppose that there might be hesitation and dithering among uniformed decision makers.

But instead, the armed services recognize the importance of actually deciding and putting a framework around it, systematizing it, reducing human error. Being decisive for decisiveness sake is not an improvement. That's the beauty of *Completed Staff Work*— it provides a process so that you're not just making a decision because it has to be made. You're making a better decision because it has been vetted.

Former General Electric CEO Jack Welch describes in *The Wall Street Journal* the Four Es of leadership where the third E is for "edge," which he describes as, "the courage to make the tough yes-or-no decisions,"

> *Look, the world is filled with gray. Anyone can look at an issue from every different angle. Some smart people can—and will— analyze those angles indefinitely. But effective people know when to stop assessing and make a tough call, even without total information.*
>
> *Little is worse than a manager who can't cut bait...*

Aristotle said, "Courage is the first virtue that makes all other virtues possible."

The manager will never have all of the information needed to stand up. He will never have enough perfect, timely data. But he must rise to the occasion and make the decision and lead.

Your Business Professor has a large poster of Ronald Reagan with George Bush in his home office. The two former presidents are pictured at a podium with upraised arms in victory. Large print across the top of the image reads,

The time
is now.

So. There I was, a newly minted Butter Bar, a Second Lieutenant, and I asked for the work as Class Leader. I was a newbie who knew nothing, of course—I had been in the Army "all day," as the joke goes; zero time in grade.

After the interview, I learned that I had received the appointment. I got the job.

I would like to report that I was selected because of my charismatic leadership and extensive knowledge of Army procedures as well as my military bearing and command presence.

No.

I got the slot because I asked for it. No one else wanted it.

My wife Charmaine worked in the Reagan White House in Presidential Personnel. This is the office in every new presidential administration tasked with placing the president's nominees throughout the government, with the express purpose of implementing the new policy agenda; it is executive recruiting and human resource management at the highest level, with national implications. President Reagan became known for the maxim that *Personnel Is Policy.* His guideline was to focus on hiring people who shared his philosophies of governance and decision-making.

He knew that the decisions are shaped long before they get to a leader's desk.

This lesson applies in government and business. The manager's life is fearlessly facing conundrums.

★

"Command focus!" the advisor kept repeating to the CEO.

It was good advice. But it's harder than it sounds. Top managers are distracted by problems and opportunities. D. Michael Lindsay, Ph.D., interviewed dozens of CEOs and then wrote about the CEO experience in *View From The Top: An Inside Look at How People in Power See and Shape the World,* observing that a consistent theme among the leaders he interviewed was the challenge of defining their focus,

> *"Every day, there were 15 things I could do that would've been rewarding…and I could only do 7 of them."*
>
> *One former governor describes his work as a "blizzard of daily information, challenges, information, questions, decisions."*
>
> *"We all have infinite jobs," one telecom executive said, "I could work 24 hours every day and never be done."*

After talking with so many CEOs, Lindsay concluded: "With so much on their plates, leaders need to have systems in place to make the most of their limited time."

"I'm down to working half-days," said the harried manager, "7 to 7." This old joke underscores the reality that management responsibility doesn't ever really end. There is always something that can be done to advance organizational goals.

Management is like housework when you have children living at home: it is neverending. Indeed, for managers there is no such thing as a clean house and an empty inbox.

Understanding the work is without end means the manager must decide what to act upon. He makes the hard, impossible decisions. He chooses.

This is why *Completed Staff Work* is so essential. Lindsay interviewed Andy Card, Chief of Staff to President George W. Bush, who said that his job was to "put out fires" so that his boss, the world's most powerful man, could focus on the decisions only he could make.

> *"I don't believe," Card said, "the president should ever make an easy decision. If the president is making an easy decision, the chief of staff probably hasn't done his or her job. Presidents make only tough decisions." (Lindsay 2014)*

As the chief of staff, Card made sure that only the biggest challenges reached the president's desk. Card gave President Bush only the tough calls. Routine and lower-risk decisions were pushed down—to be made by people further south in the hierarchy. The manager decides at which level some decisions are made.

And it would appear that is the challenge for managers and stockholders. Younger workers today, not really needing money or security, are moving up on Maslow's hierarchy of needs, challenging any corporate organization chart on their way to becoming self-actualized beings.

These days, structure is out. Bootlicking is out.

If there were no problems, or no change of any kind, or no exciting opportunities to compete for capital budget allocation, there would be no need for that overhead known as "the Manager."

The Democracy replacing Bureaucracy experiment usually doesn't work. The reasons are easily explained.

We are all equal in the eyes of the Creator or under the law and the blind eyes of Justice. But we are not equal to one another. Egalitarianism of this sort is for Marxists and the French. Not for the pursuit of a customer and profit. Sorry.

The manager may not be able to fire an employee for incompetence these days, but he can fire for insubordination. Or he might be tasked with reducing headcount; maybe to improve cash flow. The manager's vote counts; yours may not. Sorry.

Democratic-egalitarian management will not work for most organizations because, sooner or later, the building will catch on fire, so to say. Emergencies will not permit much discussion, or consensus, or a vote tally. Sometimes there isn't time.

And someone has to be in charge. There must be a captain of the ship.

And even if the building is not burning, too much time-consuming "consensus building" is exhausting for the manager and paralyzing to the organization. The wise manager can do the balancing.

President Bill Clinton famously had enormous meetings with adoring staff; each participant partici-panting ideologues. The meetings ran long. Clinton ran late. Nothing got done.

Clinton was noted for his reacting, not acting or not taking a position and deciding. The effective organization is not a headless democracy. There is often not a direct vote on a decision, but there is input. The manager should demand staffer recommendations and the individual contributors should expect to deliver them.

The best organizations appoint a manager as decision-maker who will use *Completed Staff Work.*

Decision is what the manager produces based on the work of the staff. The origin of the word "decision" means "to cut" and the boss cuts out alternatives. Management is defined as plan, organize, lead, and control. Each of the four parts should involve making a decision made by the boss. The staffer recommends; the manager decides.

Discussion Questions
1. Can the science of management be taught? Explain.
2. Does the manager limit his opportunities when cutting out options?

3. Is the manager still necessary in today's world of knowledge workers?
4. If your decisions are easy, are you valuable to the organization? Why?
5. Under what circumstances are we equal or not equal to one another?
6. What does the manager do?
7. What is a conundrum?

CHAPTER 3

Finished: The recommendation is complete; there is nothing to add.

ROBERT MOSES WAS PREPARED. HIS team had the blueprints rolled up and ready to go. The building permits would not be a problem. The workforce was identified. His projects were, as we say in my generation, "shovel ready."

It was the Great Depression and millions were out of work. In the early 1930s, President Roosevelt used government funding to build public works to create jobs. In New York City money was available to put men back to work.

The federal government administrators asked leaders in cities across the country to submit proposals for building projects using the armies of unemployed and millions of tax dollars. And the states sent their local administrators to the federal decision-makers with ideas on how to put men and money to good use.

They all had great ideas. The studies and designs and estimates would be started as soon as they got the monetary grants.

Robert Moses had more than good intentions. His projects got funded. The others—not so much.

Moses had all the preliminary groundwork done. His team marched down the marble halls of government buildings with bulging briefing books. They would make a presentation, agreements would be signed, and a check would follow.

Others had an outline. Moses had *Completed Staff Work*. He won the contracts.

In his epic bestseller *The Power Broker*, historian Robert Caro tells the story of Robert Moses, who is known for building NYC's infrastructure. Moses got things done because his staff, his "Moses Men" anticipated every need to begin and finish vast public works projects. He was not always popular. But he got things done.

★

Completed Staff Work is a finished product where the staffer works and the manager decides.

Managers often complain that their direct reports are running out of work while the manager is running out of time.

But this is not always the fault of the individual contributor. Sometimes the manager does not know what direction, what procedure to give his direct reports.

Managers know that their job is to Plan, Organize, Lead, and Control. And so they plunge in. With a typically aggressive American work ethic. However, managers often end up working too hard—thinking that working "hard" is how the "lead" part of management is defined.

But ironically, their good intentions may be exactly what is sabotaging their leadership effectiveness. For talented managers, the "leading" part of management might be the easiest. When the manager has *Completed Staff Work*, the staff does the work and the manager makes the decision.

This is what it looks like. A problem or opportunity is presented by the manager or uncovered by the staff. However the assignment originates, the staffer using *Completed Staff Work* follows this simple three-step outline that we introduced in chapter 1:

- Performs the research exploring the landscape for nearly all possible possibilities.
- Develops a number of likely options, scenarios, and solutions.
- Finalizes and presents (sells) a recommendation.

The Alert Manager will note that the manager did little work in this phase. The staff does the labor. It is complete. The boss can accept or reject or modify the recommendation. But usually the manager will simply adopt the staff recommendation. When *Completed Staff Work* is done correctly the manager is left with only signing his name making a decision. This is why "leadership" can be simple.

Scripture has a reference to the completed work of Jesus Christ, on the cross. John 19:30 records Christ's last words, *It is finished.* Biblical scholars tell us that the more accurate translation is, "It has been finished." The verb tense, intensive perfect passive, tells us that the action was completed in the past, was seen at the crucifixion, and can be read now. The work is finished and nothing can be added to it.

This would be, well, the ultimate *Completed Staff Work.*

If the reader were a present-day General Lerch or a Moses Man, how would he know when his Staff Work is Completed? The staffer's recommendation might well be a finished product if it could survive the "Kissinger Challenge." Demand the best: don't read an unfinished first draft.

Exasperated managers often complain about substandard staff work. Reports will not have enough detail or, worse, too much. The concern for managers is to train staffers to deliver *Completed Staff Work*. They might take a lesson from Harvard professor and President Richard Nixon's Secretary of State, Henry Kissinger.

Ambassador Winston Lord tells a story, archived by George Washington University, about what it was like to work for Kissinger, and the level of excellence and preparation that he demanded. When he was a young man, Lord says,

> *I would go in with a draft of the speech. [Kissinger] called me in the next day and said, "Is this the best you can do?" I said, "Henry, I thought so, but I'll try again."*
>
> *So I go back in a few days, another draft. He called me in the next day and he said, "Are you sure this is the best you can do?"*
>
> *I said, "Well, I really thought so. I'll try one more time."*
>
> *Anyway, this went on eight times, eight drafts; each time he said, "Is this the best you can do?" So I went in there with a ninth draft, and when he called me in the next day and asked me that same question, I really got exasperated and I said, "Henry, I've beaten my brains out— this is the ninth draft. I know it's the best I can do: I can't possibly improve one more word."*
>
> *He then looked at me and said, "In that case, now I'll read it."*

The manager can help get a finished recommendation from his Individual Contributors by using a clever mnemonic shortcut. Consultant and former Director of Corporate Planning for Washington Water Power Company, Dr. George T. Doran, wrote about S.M.A.R.T. objectives in 1981.

Specific – target
Measurable – quantify
Assignable – who

Realistic — sensible

Time-related — when

The staffer's recommendation to his boss should include the functions of management on which the leader must decide: what to do, how much, who does it, is it possible, and the time constraints.

Of the goals, time-related might the most important of the four. For example, historian William Manchester writes about General Douglas MacArthur and the need for timing. Manchester describes the years shortly before the outbreak of World War II when MacArthur wrote in despair:

> *"The history of failure in war can be summed up in two words: Too Late. Too late in comprehending the deadly purpose of a potential enemy; too late in realizing the mortal danger; too late in preparedness; too late in uniting all possible forces for resistance; too late in standing with one's friends." (Manchester, 1978)*

Recommendations and decisions must be timely.

The four goals, specific, measurable, assignable, and realistic, should also be seen in the finished product. A simple example is a letter of recommendation.

Your Business Professor has written dozens of recommendations for hundreds of students, clients, friends, and vendors.

Question: If I wrote dozens of letters, then how did hundreds of people get a written recommendation?

Answer: I didn't write them.

I used to write recommendations all the time. Before I got smart. (This took a long time.) I once received a glowing recommendation from a United States congressman for a presidential appointment. It was fantastic; the glowing language, the detailed biography, the compelling argument. To read the letter one might ask, "Wow!

That congressman must really know Jack! Were they roommates in college? Are they cousins? Did they serve jail time together?"

Nope. The Good Congressman hardly knew me to send me anything other than a Christmas card. No, the Good Congressman didn't actually write my recommendation.

I did.

I didn't dare impose upon The Very Important Person to write a gushing letter of endorsement. I assigned it not to the Congressman, but to me: I self-delegated.

Why did a Very Busy Big Boss sign-off on a letter to Your (little known) Business Professor?

A trusted third party.

To get a recommendation from a Very Busy Big Boss— a decision, a signature—you need *Completed Staff Work*. Find a contact whom the Boss trusts, a trusted mutual friend. With input from the trusted staffer, I composed a draft of my recommendation, which was fact-checked and spell-checked, of course, and signature-ready for the Big Endorser's okay.

This is important: Very Important Busy People don't have time to write *anything*. They have staff who ghostwrite their speeches. If you want an endorsement or a recommendation, you need to become a speechwriter for your own content. The letter should tell a realistic story with specifics and measurable results.

A simple story in a one-page letter would have three acts. The first act would describe a problem; the second, would explain a solution; and the final act would detail the results.

The story would be complete.

This is the first lesson in *Completed Staff Work* for subordinates. The Big Boss should only make decisions and sign his name. The Boss does not do any work; that is, "work" in the form that the normal individual contributor or staffer would recognize.

I tell Interested Parties if they want my written recommendation on why someone should hire them—the Interested Party must first draft the letter so that I would know why I would make such a suggestion.

Someone is going to have to do the thinking and the work for me. This is how senior management thinks.

Some Interested Parties might suggest that Your Business Professor is not very bright and certainly very lazy. Perhaps so. But.

This is how senior management works and gets things done through *Completed Staff Work.*

Finished: is where the recommendation is a finished product, there is nothing to add. The "work" of the manager is different from the work of the individual staffer. The staffer offers a refined, completed recommendation that only requires the signature of the manager. The manager might make minor adjustments but the work is done.

Discussion Questions
1. Why was Robert Moses able to get so much done?
2. *Completed Staff Work* is a finished product. Explain.
3. Why does *Completed Staff Work* make managing simple?
4. What is a SMART goal? Give an example.
5. What is the "Kissinger Challenge"?

CHAPTER 4

Deputy: Every manager needs a back-up to stand-in.

THE UNIT WAS RUNNING PERFECTLY. So why was the boss unhappy?

The officer-in-charge was miffed. He went on leave, and when he returned from his vacation he complained that:

> *It evidently made no difference whether I was there to look after things or not.*
>
> *I had imagined that the condition of the cars, whether or not things were obtainable, the smooth functioning of the business of removing wounded and sick from the dressing stations, hauling them back from the mountains to the clearing station, and then distributing them to the hospitals named on their papers, depended to a considerable extent on myself.*
>
> *Evidently it did not matter whether I [as the manager] was there or not.*

Ernest Hemingway was writing about the Italian campaign in World War One in *A Farewell to Arms* published after the war in 1929. He unwittingly told a story of what a deputy's job looks like in *Completed Staff Work*. As a young lieutenant, Hemingway didn't quite know how professional management really worked. He had a second-in-command and a competent team in place. In his extended absence, they had executed delegated tasks effectively.

This is every manager's fantasy.

Most teams will deliver when the boss is a clear and present danger to malingerers. However, the best teams work best *not* when the boss is present, but where the manager's influence is omnipresent. The manager's 'presence' exists even in his absence.

How is this done?

Get a deputy. This person can have a variety of titles: Chief-of-Staff, Executive Officer, Executive Assistant, First Mate, Second Banana, or Sidekick. You may even hear that politically incorrect term Girl Friday.

The best managers identify and groom staff with promotion potential to train for the role of deputy or acting boss. The deputy does what the manager would do if he or she had unlimited hours in the day.

The deputy gets the job done even when the boss is on vacation.

"Leadership," says writer and speaker Ken Blanchard, "is not just what happens when you're there, it's what happens when you're not there."

The job of a deputy is to assist the manager and give him that most precious of commodities: time to think. The boss must train and mentor a deputy for two reasons.

First, the deputy can step up into the role if the manager moves or is moved out of the top slot. This succession management ensures the primary goal of the business, which is the survival of the firm as an ongoing entity.

Second, like Andy Card, the deputy is deputized to handle "little" decisions, saving the boss only the Big Ones.

Lists are helpful. The U.S. Army publishes the (unclassified; I think) *Commander and Staff Office Guide* detailing *common staff duties and responsibilities*,

1. Advising and informing the commander.
2. Building and maintaining running estimates.
3. Providing recommendations.
4. Preparing plans, order, and other staff writing.
5. Assessing operations.
6. Managing information within area of expertise.
7. Identifying and analyzing problems.
8. Coordinating staff.
9. Conducting staff assistance visits.
10. Performing composite risk management.
11. Performing intelligence preparation of the battlefield.
12. Conducting staff inspections.
13. Completing staff research.
14. Performing staff administrative procedures.
15. Exercising staff supervision over their area of expertise.

This is a lot of work. This list includes only a small number of the many responsibilities of every manager, regardless of the size of the department or company. The only variable between two business units would be the number of zeros (in the budget, not those empty placeholders in the headcount).

The presidential chief of staff under George H.W. Bush, John Sununu, recounts a story of a foreign policy crisis that required a recommendation from the President's advisors—and gives a window into the deputy's role in *Completed Staff Work*,

[National Security Advisor] Scowcroft and I were getting frequent updates by phone. We learned that the rebels had seized some facilities and were threatening to attack the Philippine presidential palace.

We were fielding calls from [Deputy National Security Advisor] Gates, [Vice President] Quayle, and [Secretary of Defense] Cheney, who were trying to formulate a reasonable response.

Eventually, the recommendation from the deputies' meeting was to fly American fighter jets over the rebel forces and the palace to demonstrate U.S. support for [Philippines president] Aquino.

The president [George H.W. Bush] and [Secretary of State] Jim Baker were both asleep. After Scowcroft and I were confident that the group had finally committed to a course of action, I woke up the president and asked him to approve the recommendation.

After thinking about it for a few moments, Bush agreed. Then he went right back to sleep. The strategy turned out to work well, and it nipped the uprising in the bud without requiring any serious intervention. (Sununu 2014)

The story is remarkable for three points:

1. The chief of staff crafted a timely recommendation.
2. The president signed-off without modification.
3. The president went back to sleep.

President Bush had such confidence in the wisdom and judgment of his team that he was able to rest assured.

How can a manager find such a deputy? That's the $64,000 question. The best answer is, by trial, a crucible.

A Biblical reference confirms this in 1 Timothy 3:10, *They must first be tested; and then if there is nothing against them, let them serve as deacons.*

Tragedy reveals; it makes a bad man worse and a good man better. Your Business Professor once worked with a prosthetist, a specialist who fabricates prosthetic devices, known as artificial limbs. His calling, his work, was to mechanically rebuild a limb and, more important, a life. He often said that how victims decide to face a tragedy made them into the best people—or the worst.

Confronting a challenge and the reaction to adversity and the decisions that follow can help in evaluating a person's character. Limbs don't have to be lost for a person to be temperamentally tested.

Sometimes the test is to lose entire countries.

The Army Chief of Staff had a simple test for his understudy. Marshall asked Eisenhower for a recommendation. Marshall wanted from Eisenhower a course of action concerning our allies in the Philippines who were about to be overrun by the Japanese Empire. The Chief of Staff was observing the younger Eisenhower,

> *Seeing if Ike had sufficient ice in his veins to recommend that thousands of his old friends and comrades in the Philippines be abandoned, condemning them to death or a war spent as prisoners of the Japanese." (Ricks, 2012)*

Marshall valued character and a team spirit above all else. But sometimes part of the team would be ignored or painfully left behind.

Eisenhower was a Brigadier General, with a single star that is the entry level into the army's highest commands. He would grow fast on the job. Ike responded in a written recommendation, "Don't be sentimental. Give up the islands, and leave American and Filipino friends there to their fate, while giving them what small aid we can. Fall back and regroup." (Ricks, 2012)

The Philippines would be lost.

Character should always be hired over intellect. In General Eisenhower, Marshall got both.

Eisenhower solved the conundrum and produced the "perfect," however painful, answer to Marshall's question. It was the least bad option. The strategic decision was made that "no Army reinforcements will be sent to the Philippine Coastal Frontier." Eisenhower would be communicating to General MacArthur that the commander would lose friends and the Philippines to the Japanese.

Eisenhower had been tested. Ike proved that he could make hard recommendations and harder decisions. Marshall gave Eisenhower more responsibility and he would later head the Allied invasion of Normandy in June of 1944. He would be promoted to five-star general and later elected president. But he started as a Deputy.

Deputy: This person does what the manager would do if he or she had unlimited time. The second-in-command or second string or second banana is the groomed understudy who can step in and can act for the manager. This trusted subordinate usually has signature authority for the boss.

Discussion Questions
1. The manager's work is never done. Explain.
2. What did Hemingway miss on management?
3. Why is an expert staffer indispensable?
4. Why is an expert manager dispensable?
5. The big boss makes big decisions. Who makes the small ones?
6. What is the value of testing?
7. Discuss a trial or obstacle you had to overcome.
8. How can your manager sleep soundly?
9. "Leadership... happens when you're not there." Explain.

CHAPTER 5

Authority: The right to act.

THE BOARD OF DIRECTORS MEETING was a success. But trouble was coming. Frank was an experienced CEO who could see a train wreck coming, he predicted, in 12 months.

Visionaries can see all kinds of things in the future. He was forecasting his own firing.

"I'm confused," says Your Business Professor. (This is a natural state for me. They would call this "typecasting" in show business.)

Anyway, involuntary termination did not look like it was in the cards. All the stats and stars were pointed and aligned in the right directions. Revenue was up. Expenses were down. Staff turnover was down. There was new demand for new products. Clients were happy. The bosses were happy.

"What's the problem?" I ask. "Your numbers are good..."

"Too good," Frank grumbles. "Nobody bothered me when I first came on board, when the numbers were lousy. But now everybody wants in on the action."

"That's a good thing, right?"

"Wrong."

"Huh?" We consultants get paid to ask the right questions. Dumb looks and mumbling, as they say, are free.

Frank says, "Sales are going to take off like a rocket and the busybodies on the board are now contacting my staff with ideas and projects and assignments and-..."

"Usually boards are criticized for not being engaged," I say.

"There's a fine line between engagement... and meddling..."

I was about to be reminded that management is best exercised when authority is transmitted down a recognized and respected chain of command.

In 1916 Henri Fayol, a French managing engineer, published a book outlining 14 Principles of Management. Professor Bateman *et. al.,* reviewed them in his popular textbook, *Management.*

The first principle was, "**Division of work**—divide work into specialized tasks and assign responsibilities to specific individuals."

His second was, "**Authority**—delegate authority along with responsibility."

The fourth on Fayol's list was, "**Unity of command**—each employee should be assigned only one supervisor."

Number nine was, "**Scalar chain**—keep communications within the chain of command." (Bateman 2012)

Frank's Directors were violating at least these four principles and probably others. The most egregious management error in board governance was the disruption of the chain of command.

The principle has been used since armies were first organized in antiquity. A clear chain of command is necessary so directions and commands can be issued down the links of the chain in the hierarchy. And accountability has a path up.

Fayol called this the Scalar chain. He used a ladder analogy where each rung is a person in the organizational chart. The rungs are a step down for orders and a step up for reporting results. The word *scalar* shares the Latin roots for "stairs" and "scale" as to climb.

★

Frank saw instantly that the board were overstepping the rungs of good management practices. "I can't manage my direct reports who get assignments from those board members reaching around me," he said. "They think that they are just trying to help…"

It wasn't malicious. But the malpractice was going to end badly, as I was beginning to learn. "You see," said Frank, "those guys on the board will tell the staff what to do and my team will get confused about their priorities. And when they don't get it right, they won't get axed—I will."

Frank continued, "And meanwhile, I'm just another direct report alongside my staff who are now taking orders from my bosses."

"Goodness," I said, "you've just been demoted."

Frank was able to avoid the train wreck. His outstanding performance landed him another CEO position just inside a year. He had seen it coming. The board members simply didn't know what they were doing.

He was still responsible for the performance of his business. But his authority was circumvented by his superiors north on the org chart.

"Flat as a pancake." The most fashionable organizational structure for trendy companies is to eliminate all middle management and de-layer the org chart. A good manager should be able to handle two dozen direct reports. Right?

Or so goes the popular conventional wisdom of modern management. However, the upper limit for a normal horizontal span of control for most concerns is a dozen. Think Jesus and the Twelve Apostles. An Army infantry square has ten men. The 1967 movie *The Dirty Dozen* is a better title than *The Dirty 19 Not Counting Support Staff…*

When a new manager is being recruited, an organization's leadership will consider what and who the manager will be managing—and where vertically in the org chart the manager will work. How much authority to grant is an essential question.

The military has devoted considerable effort to study this challenge.

Author and CEO Kevin Kruse summarizes the Army's field manual (FM 22-100) on leadership and tactical management and divides the governance into three categories: Direct, Organizational, and Strategic. The military text has gone through a number of editions since Your Business Professor was pinned with the gold bar insignia as a Second Lieutenant. Here's what the three categories look like.

Managers. These are the first line supervisors with direct contact with the individual contributors. The individual contributors are the staffers who do the doing: an accountant working a spreadsheet, an actor on stage, a salesman with a customer, a truck driver, or bricklayer. The manager, or coach, foreman, team leader, shift supervisor, communicates directly, most often face-to-face. The staff usually consists of hourly workers with a short-time horizon for production goals—day to day, or week to week, or month to month. These immediate managers are subject matter experts in the work of the direct reports. Their report card will answer the question, "What does success look like this month?"

Managers of managers. These managers plan, organize, lead, and control a team not of individual contributors, but of managers. The span of control in each of the three categories is about ten people. The manager of a team of ten who manages ten down-line teams of ten, then has up to an army of 100. This modern centurion leads a team of teams under a longer timeline of months to perhaps a year. The decision-making is on procedures. Their report card will answer the question, "What does success look like this year?"

Managers of the organization. Here, the managers decide policy for the strategic direction of a company. At the top of the hierarchal pyramid the talent needed is the exercise of influence. Here the leader can command his direct reporting managers but he can only indirectly influence and persuade the employees deeper in the org chart. The CEO's influence should also extend beyond the organization to other enterprises.

The military calls this unity "jointness." Civilians call this "collaboration." Jack Welch aptly described this working together as "boundaryless" at GE. The senior leadership team sets the vision of the organization. The direction and timeline is years into the future. The CEO's report card examines the question, "What does success look like five years from now?"

Different levels of management require different skills in leadership and limits in authority. These limits must have clear and visible boundaries. Or there will be confusion.

"You have the assignment?" I said to the guy running legal. "I thought I had the assignment." I was running human resources.

We both were given the same task by our mutual Big Boss VP who was layered above us at the Organizational Olympus.

We only found out about the dual/duplication delegation when we began dueling for resources to do the job. Our boss gave each of us the same mission and did not coordinate our efforts. We found that support staff was doing the same work reporting on the work-product progress up two divergent chains of command.

We were both given the authority. And we both had the responsibility.

This does not have a happy ending.

It was something like a matrix structure where one person or team reports to two different managers.

Except that no single point of contact was in charge. There were two. The relationships were not doubled but, multiplied exponentially.

This was a reporting structure even more unmanageable. The Big Boss failed to understand this variation of the principle of Unity of Command where authority flowed down the organization. The one boss should hold one person accountable for one task.

Peter Thiel writes in *Zero to One: Notes on Startups, or How to Build the Future,*

> *The best thing I did as a manager at PayPal was to make every person in the company responsible for doing just one thing.*
>
> *But then I noticed a deeper result: defining roles reduced conflict. Most fights inside a company happen when colleagues compete for the same responsibilities.*
>
> *Startups face an especially high risk of this since job roles are fluid at the early stages. Eliminating competition makes it easier for everyone to build the kinds of long-term relationships that transcend mere professionalism. (Thiel, 2014)*

The U.S. Army would agree with Silicon Valley,

> *Each mission requires only a single tactical action, and the commander employs tactics to accomplish each. (Army Doctrine Publication 2011)*
>
> *Unified action is the synchronization, coordination, and/or integration of the activities of governmental and nongovernmental entities with military operations to achieve unity of effort. (Operations FM-03, 2008)*

The civilian world doesn't much like hard, callous military words like "command" preferring the more inclusive "unity of effort."

But the principle is the same.

The Big Boss VP squandered the resources of his team. He failed in the "organize" part of management of who-does-what with his teams' bifurcated efforts.

Within a year he lost his ability to lead; he lost his power to inspire. In two years he lost his authority to lead; he got fired.

He might have been able to keep his job if he understood how authority was exercised and if he was accountable to a higher authority on the conduct of his work.

I am a certified brake mechanic. Your Business Professor is rather proud of this accomplishment. However, this seems to make no impression in the faculty lounges in academia.

Years ago, I instructed auto mechanics on brake repairs. I knew my stuff (or "content" as we call it nowadays) but it mattered little what I claimed. The American Society of Engineers evaluated my knowledge and *they* said that I knew what I was doing. The ASE is a respected, nongovernmental, private association that provides credentials proving competence. Mechanics may—or may not—have trusted me, but they trusted the ASE.

Relationships often need a third-party validation. I can claim competence. A mother can claim competence for her child. But we might have biased opinions of self and offspring.

Outside parties like the Better Business Bureau and the ASE have the authority granted by their ruling Boards of Directors and their membership to recognize my fitness and to enforce business ethics as a condition for admission.

The ancient Jews did not have the United Nations or Better Business Bureau. They had to rely on an even higher authority.

God.

The Old Testament story is told of Laban and his son-in-law Jacob, whom God renamed "Israel." The two resolved a dispute and were to part in friendly company. They built a mound of stones and a pillar to commemorate the agreement. Jacob named the place, noted in Genesis 31:49; *It was also called Mizpah, because he said, "May the LORD keep watch between you and me when we are away from each other…"*

The rocks were to be boundary stones and the memorial at Mizpah was known as "Watchtower." Laban and Jacob were both accountable to the ultimate higher ruling authority: The Creator.

"Mizpah" can represent the emotional connection, the bond between two individuals while they are apart. It is popularized by jewelry. The Mizpah Coin is cut in two with each half worn by a separated couple. It is also seen on headstones.

However, the common usage seems to be a gentle reminder or a lighthearted encouragement between lovers. Originally, it was no such thing. *May the LORD keep watch* is actually a dire warning to demand compliance to the agreement and to be subordinate to the Ultimate Authority.

The contract at Mizpah was serious business in a three-way relationship: The Eternal, Omnipotent Boss, Laban, and Jacob. The authority of a third-party certification today serves in a similar way.

Authority is the right to make decisions in an organization. Here the manager, as author-creator, bestows the mantle, the signet ring, the corner office, or the sergeant's stripes onto his subordinate. The junior staffer cannot claim authority for himself; it is only granted by a higher authority from a higher position in the organization. However, granting authority does not guarantee that power will follow.

THE MEMO

Discussion Questions
1. Is it possible to report to two or more managers? Why?
2. How are Henri Fayol and Peter Thiel similar?
3. Explain the work of the three levels of management
4. Does Authority give Power? Explain.
5. What is the value of certification?
6. What is the chain of command?
7. How can disputes be resolved between two departments?
8. What is a span of control?

CHAPTER 6

Power: The ability to influence.

AS THE STORY IS TOLD, John Adams, the second president of the United States, was having a meal with his vice president, Thomas Jefferson.

They were discussing how to prevent a war and how to manage unpredictable factors that would influence foreign countries abroad, and voters here at home.

John Adams said, "I am determined to control events, not be controlled by them."

This is presidential.

Anyone can be a victim of circumstance; it doesn't require a senior pay-grade or a national election. Presidents and CEOs, and even newly minted managers, don't get paid to be happenstance victims of outrageous fortune.

Controlling events means that we so anticipate what can happen in any event that we will have a fallback position, an alternate route, a plan B.

Just like David did when facing Goliath.

Then he...chose five smooth stones from the stream, put them in the pouch of his shepherd's bag and, with his sling in his hand, approached the Philistine. (1 Samuel 17:40)

David knew he could handle Goliath with a single stone, and that he did. So why did he pick up five stones? Why the margin, the excess capacity and the extra combat load? He didn't think that he would miss his target—so what was he thinking?

David was going to control events no matter what the Giant, or his family, would do. Goliath had four brothers and David did not know how the giant's kin would react to the rival of their sibling. Five potential adversaries. Five stones.

David was not going to wait and see and hope. He would be ready with any decision his opponent(s) made. David was not going to be controlled by outside circumstances. He would be ready.

CEOs make things happen. They control events.

To control events, a leader must exercise power. The most formidable skill anyone can have is the ability to influence, to persuade.

All managers have authority, but not all have power.

I saw this first and most vividly in the Army. Captain Blunder had the authority but little power. First Lieutenant Crisp, his executive officer or second in command, had less authority but had great power.

Captain Blunder could only get things done with a direct order relying on his rank and position as company commander. He was slow to take recommendations from his staff. He embodied the old saying—he kissed up and kicked down.

First Lt. Crisp got things done with persuasion and influence. He actively sought out recommendations. Crisp seldom said "I." He spoke in the second person plural, "Here's what we need to do." Most of all, he listened to his sergeants. He had power. His boss did not.

A primary lesson for managers in getting *Completed Staff Work* from their team is knowing when to give a directive (using authority) and when to gently persuade (using power). The seasoned CEO fully understands the difference between power and authority. The professional knows that positions have authority, while people have power.

Management books segment the different kinds of power. Mark Horstman, the producer of the "Manager Tools" podcast, offers an outline of three different kinds of power: Positional, Relational, and Expertise.

First is **Positional** or **Legitimate Power** where a third party, recognized by all the varied stakeholders, appoints a person to a position. For example, a pope would crown a medieval king. The Archbishop of Canterbury presides over the coronation ceremony of the monarch of the United Kingdom. An important part of Positional Power is the Reward Power, where the manager has the ability to allocate pay raises or perquisites ("perks"). This power could be delegated to a person, manager or not, who has control over a bag of goodies to dispense. Positional Power comes from "where" you are on the org chart.

The second power is **Relational**, which are the connections and intersections a powerful person has developed over time. Are your phone calls returned? Email promptly answered? No matter where you sit on the org chart, that's power. It has been said that it's *not what you know*, it's the *people you know*—and the addendum of, *who knows you*. Indeed, the word "Relationship" describes management. But also networks should be expanded by individual contributors to build and strengthen relationships.

The third type of power is **Expertise**, based on your occupational competency or the "what" you know. This is the Go-To, Answer Man who can *Git-R-Done* as Larry the Cable Guy would say. His knowledge is right, on time and without doubt. This power is usually in the domain of the individual contributor.

Corporal Radar O'Reilly had no Positional power, but he did have Relational and Expertise influence. He is the patron saint of *Completed Staff Work*; even though he was an unassuming television character—but still a genius. As *People* magazine noted,

> *During his seven-year stint as the sensitive Cpl. Walter "Radar" O'Reilly on the hit TV show M*A*S*H, Gary Burghoff played a character who was a model of military precision.*
> *"Radar was the one who could get things done," says Larry Gelbart, executive producer of the Korean War series, which aired from 1972 to 1983. "You had the feeling he made the camp run."*

Every organization and every manager would be lucky if there were at least one "Radar" on staff.

New managers need to learn the value of the power of relationships and experience. They will often incorrectly assume that authority comes solely from the position they hold. They expect the position itself to give them the power to command effectively. The amateur assumes that power will be conveyed with a new position as The Boss. The pro knows that being the boss does not automatically bestow power.

Let's not miss the key feature of Radar's effectiveness: the Colonel listened to him. He may have blustered, but ultimately, he took Radar's suggestions. *Completed Staff Work* as a system depends on the manager and staff working as a cohesive whole.

The manager sets the priorities for the staff, of course. The boss sets the target and the policy but should allow the staffers some flexibility in the procedures. And here's where the leadership component of management comes in.

As a young Armored Cavalry Officer, Your Business Professor, was confidently directing the direction of my light tanks when my Platoon Sergeant (my deputy) gently recommended another route.

My course of travel was the more efficient and more direct (of course!). But the wizened soldier mentioned that our team did not know the route conditions of the road I had proposed and they were most familiar with an alternate route. Because they knew well the road they wanted to take, the trip might very well be faster. And they would be motivated to make sure that no vehicles "got stuck" or "broke down."

My soldiers would never, never break down deliberately, to be sure. But accidents do happen. Especially to Managers Who Know Everything.

The tank drivers were hot, that is, more confident on their known route, and lukewarm about my plan. It really made no difference to me or the mission (since I really didn't know what I was doing anyway) so I granted the change. This made for happy trails.

My team had strong opinions on the course of action and let me know about it.

What my sergeant was doing was advising me that a course of action is more easily completed when the team has some input on how get there. Consultants call this "empowerment." Catholic social teaching calls this "subsidiarity."

I call it "lucky." The Army had assigned an experienced Non-Commissioned Officer, lower-ranking but with Expertise Power, to train-up this young lieutenant (me) with Positional Power.

The platoon arrived at our destination on time with no problems and no injuries. Every manager should have such luck.

★

On an island off Greece in the Second World War, the Italian army had a Radar O'Reilly-like mastermind in one of their military depots, repairing tracked and wheeled vehicles. The mechanic, Ferruccio, was a genius. He had an uncanny instinct for knowing how to fix even the newest machinery that came into his motor pool. Every commander on that island was dependent upon supervisor Ferruccio and his mechanical magic. He knew the 'how-to' and became the 'go-to.' He was a powerful Expert.

However, his power diverged from Radar's in a significant way. After the war, Ferruccio explained how he had so impressed the chain of command with his specialized knowledge. He said, "My ability was largely due to having been the first person on the island to receive the repair manuals, which I memorized and then destroyed so as to become indispensable." (Robbins 2010)

Organizing has been defined as, "The management function of assembling and coordinating human, financial, physical, informational, and other resources needed to achieve goals." Managers can best organize when knowledge is available across business silos. This is what Jack Welch calls "boundarylessness' that we discussed in chapter five, or "jointness" as Marine Corps General John J. Sheehan said in 1996. (Defense.gov 2014)

William A. Cohen, Ph.D., a retired major (two-star) general in the Air Force, reminds us of the need for selfless collaboration. Cohen uses the famous Peter Drucker as an example,

> Peter Drucker was…a unique genius. Drucker was in a class with Newton, Freud and Einstein, and like them Peter wanted to see his insights and conclusions disseminated and applied. (Cohen 2012)

Ferruccio, the Italian manager, was no Peter Drucker.

After the war, Ferruccio returned to his hometown near Bologna and opened a shop. He is best known by his last name and that of his automobile company, Lamborghini.

This luxury high-performance car manufacturer has gone through bankruptcy and through a series of owners including Chrysler (!). Lamborghini is currently owned, as of this writing, by Audi AG.

And of course, as the world remembers, Italy and its ally, Germany lost in WWII. Can we blame a Ferruccio-mindset? Perhaps.

Your Business Professor was in a new car showroom in the late 1980s drooling over the Lamborghini Countach. The salesman would not let me sit in the angular 12-cylinder mid-engine monster-masterpiece. "You're too tall," he said. "The steering wheel does not adjust." It was a polite blow-off. It might even have been true.

In the tradition of Ferruccio Lamborghini, one never knows.

> *Neither do people light a lamp and put it under a bowl.*
> *Instead they put it on its stand, and it gives light to everyone in the house. (Matthew 5:15)*

It has been said that scars are tattoos with better stories.

Finding, or being assigned a beneficent guide, truly is lucky because sometimes we're left with pain as our teacher. Sometimes, you lose the war, lose the contract, lose the job. In the power game, sometimes—often—you lose.

Power comes from listening. From encouraging the Expertise of your team even when mistakes are made. Erring in the exercise of power teaches us a humility that, in a leader who has matured, leads back to listening, appreciating and crediting the contribution of others. Regardless of where they sit on the organization chart. Thucydides, the ancient Athenian historian, is credited with the observation that, "Of all manifestations of power, restraint impresses men most."

Power is the ability to influence. The best managers (with authority) and staff (without authority) can both wield power. This is the ability to persuade from any position in the organization chart. It is independent of authority and job description. Power cannot be given; it is earned and exercised.

Discussion Questions
1. All managers have authority but not all have power. Explain.
2. What is the difference between power and authority?
3. Discuss the various types of power.
4. We should control events. But can we control the weather? Discuss.
5. Ferruccio Lamborghini had power. How?

CHAPTER 7

Followership: Getting the organization⁺s priorities done.

YOUR BUSINESS PROFESSOR ONCE WORKED as a dance instructor (I was young and I needed the money). You name it, I did it—the waltz, ballroom, all the "hand-dancing."

And disco.

Please don't hate me.

Followership is dancing with the leadership of an organization, if not dancing with the stars. In this chapter, dance instruction meets the practice of management. Follow these steps for an interpretation of hands-on management: Practice Frame, Firm with Fun.

Frame. Dancing with a partner starts with a "frame." This is the simple structure of where hands go. There is actual human contact here (not always recommended with your manager). When learning to dance, the next moves, the dance steps, are first learned and rehearsed without music. Using the frame, there is a great deal of communication between dance partners, but not much is verbal.

The follower is not a passive sheep, blindly following the shepherd-leader. The follower is engaged. He is not alienated. He is, well, a partner in execution. Competence and compliance in followership and dancing follow simple rules.

Firm. The framing between dance partners is nearly rigid. A common mistake seen in dance training is when both the leader and follower have "spaghetti arms." But dancing, like all human interaction, needs a solid connection. Secure—there is no floppy disco. The following partner will offer a confident push back, which gives the dance leader confidence of a solid construction.

Leaders need to know where the follower is and is going. The partner knows the commander's intent and can anticipate what his next move will be. The best followers are a step ahead.

Fun. After a short lesson on the rules of the road, the music is brought up and the dancers are lined up. There is much laughter and many missteps. ("I dance on the bottoms of my feet—you dance on the tops...") A bit of practice is needed, but soon the following partner easily predicts the direction that the dance team will take across the ballroom.

Followership done right can take the team across the dance floor—or across Europe.

"I was with Patton's Third Army; we rolled across France." A few decades ago the old soldier was showing me his medals from World War II. "We would follow him anywhere." He did not need to be ordered.

Military command is an exercise in compliance and initiative. General Patton could command confidence and command an army into battle. His men followed him.

Real power and real influence commands more than the body. Leadership commands the passions. Military leadership is often mocked and denigrated for the misperception of the ease of getting things done. give an order, men salute and then obey.

Instant compliance is indeed a key component of the armed services. This is understood in the giving of directions under pressure without time for debate. But the civilian should note the language and the wording: we often read about "military leadership" and less of "military management."

Real leadership, in and out of the military, is a skill of persuasion and earning the respect of subordinates. Leadership in a command position will have the right, indeed, the authority to command. A person can have the rank or a senior slot on an organizational chart, but will he be able to get things done through other people?

General and President Dwight Eisenhower said, "I would rather try to persuade a man to go along, because once I have persuaded him, he will stick. If I scare him, he will stay just as long as he is scared, then he is gone." (Fishman 2001)

A CEO will have subordinates but that does not mean he has any followers.

Ken Blanchard, author of *The One Minute Manager*, tells us,

> *I told the consultants Tom Peters and Robert Waterman, who wrote In Search of Excellence, "You didn't invent management by wandering around. Jesus did." He wandered from one little town to another, and people would say, "How do you become first?" Jesus said, "By being last."*
>
> *People would ask him, "How do you lead?"*
> *"By following."*
> *Managing the journey of change is servant leadership. We must get our egos out of the way and praise, redirect, reprimand—anything it takes to help people win.*

The most effective leader must be a humble, faithful follower. Randy Yeager, Ph.D. and a Baptist theologian, writes,

"True greatness is found in the lowest, not the highest place.
Jesus did not say, "Be a dictator."
He said, "Be a deacon."

Yeager further explains that the word *diakonos* is used in the original Greek passage and is sometimes translated as slave. It is the origin of the word "deacon," which means servant, minister, or messenger. (Yeager 1981) ...*and whoever wants to be first must be slave of all.* Mark 10:44.

Parenthood might be sweetest slavery of all.

"I want you to be proud of me!"

His little voice stopped me. I was yelling at my boy John for some minor infraction of the house rules and I let the little guy have it. But his response brought me up short. His protest, his defense, and his explanation were compelling. The little tyke was four years old.

He was remorseful, to be sure, but he was communicating to me that he was more upset about falling out of favor. He was afraid of the distance my actions were putting between us. He felt that I was mentally pushing him away. He wanted his behavior to make me proud.

How could this happen? Here's my son whom I love unconditionally in my every thought and action. And he still didn't feel valued.

I didn't let him know how important he is. I didn't "manage" the relationship very well.

Many managers don't manage well. A key reason that employees leave an organization is that they don't feel appreciated. But people just don't leave a building or a company; they leave one particular manager.

Conversely people will work for and follow a certain manager—a unique person. Just as Jesus made clear: *Come to Me.* He didn't say come to the Faith; to buy-in to that Big Org Chart in the Sky. Jesus said, *Follow Me.*

No, we are not children at work craving the attention of a boss (who thinks he's Jesus).

Sometimes we all just need to be thanked.

Peggy Noonan was a speechwriter for President Ronald Reagan, who was known as the Great Communicator. He once praised one of her drafts by writing "Very Good" in the margin.

In our house, when we got such recognition we would clip it to the refrigerator—or in some cases, even frame the attagirl and hang it over the fireplace. Peggy has more of a sense of humor (and humility). As she tells the story, she simply cut out the words and taped them on her blouse like a well-earned battle ribbon. She walked a little taller all day. She wanted to make him proud.

Peggy didn't get a pay raise. But she would step up and do anything for The Gipper.

"Never volunteer" is an old Army truism. The reasoning is simple: you won't get paid more. Competence will only increase your workload. You won't get a higher rank. Keep low. Keep quiet. Keep a low profile and do as little as possible outside of your immediate duties. You can't get hammered if you don't get noticed. No mistakes are made if nothing is moving.

This is, of course, a lie.

Every school semester, Your Business Professor tells the students that they will each introduce themselves to the class. I give them a few minutes to collect their thoughts.

Then I ask for volunteers. I wait. And wait. I know to be patient and to outwait them because no student has ever jumped in and immediately volunteered.

After an embarrassing silence, one brave soul will reluctantly volunteer to go first. This is after realizing that a long, silent, boring class will follow unless somebody says something. Because it won't be me, Your Business Professor, who is patiently waiting while the class sits mute.

As soon as the student is recognized and speaks, I interrupt him. Rudely. But I do this with a smile. I go into didactic mode and launch a lecture. (Sometimes I create my own "teachable moments." This is something best left to professionals.)

I congratulate and compliment the heroic pupil. My message is to "Always Volunteer." Stand up and go first, especially in a forum where everyone will be required to participate. Since everyone will have a speaking part, speak up and get going. There are several advantages to making the first move.

1. No one is paying any attention to the First Person. The rest of the class is rehearsing their lines that they now know that they will have to give.
2. The standard for acceptable performance is low. No one can be critical of the early speakers—who are likely to be forgotten as the others drone on. Let's call it the First Mover Advantage.
3. The followers will take the early cues and add and expand on previous speakers.
4. Finally, remember: no one is listening to the first guy anyway. He will be quickly forgotten by everyone. Except me. He will get an A in the class and he doesn't know it yet. I can make things like that happen. I am the boss.

Remember that the Faithful Follower has a constituency of one: his manager. Always be that team member who responds to the manager's request. Even if the supervisor needs only one staffer and the other nine slackers soon melt away, volunteer. You will not need to be perfect—the boss just needs some help. Be that person.

Dr. Henry Mintzberg in his book *Management* quotes Jonathan Gosling, University of Exeter, U.K., on standing up,

> *The best way to predict who will take initiative and serve as a leader is to see what young people do at school. Participating in sports, school clubs and volunteering in the community are all strongly correlated with activism in later life. Strengthening our youth organizations is a real and proven way of growing leadership... (Mintzberg 2010)*

Or, I would argue, of growing followership. Which leads to, well, leadership. Volunteers are natural leaders. Always volunteer. *Then I heard the voice of the Lord saying, "Whom shall I send? And who will go for us?" And I said, "Here am I. Send me!"* Isaiah 6:8

Leaders today have an overload of information and options. This is not good for the manager or the team. It is harder to make good decisions. Anticipating staff can act as a filter to separate the valuable "signal" from the distracting "noise." Managers need mature researchers to gather, analyze, and consider options and then to make a signature-ready recommendation. Leaders do not have time to do these tasks. This takes organizational training.

The team will be most effective by studying this contradiction:

Servant Leadership – leading by serving
Managing Servanthood – serving by leading

Followership is the exercise of leading from behind the manager or team-leader. A good follower is a good leader in the exercise of power. This is the ability to get things done through a manager, through the organization even without a position of authority. Followers provide active support to and for their managers. The art and craft of Leadership is learned in Followership.

Discussion Questions
1. How is management like dancing?
2. Why is persuasion effective?
3. *Whoever wants to be first must be slave of all* can describe management. Explain.
4. Can a manager command staff to follow him?
5. Discuss an incident where your efforts were appreciated.
6. Why volunteer in the workplace?
7. What is the value in filtering information for the manager?

PART TWO:

Problem—Why Is There
a Need for *Completed
Staff Work?*

CHAPTER 8

Effective: This is the result of the manager*s work.

The knowledge worker cannot be supervised closely or in detail. He can only be helped. But he must direct himself, and he must direct himself toward performance and contribution, that is, toward effectiveness. (Drucker, 1967)

RAYMOND DUNN, JR. WAS BORN in 1975 with a skull fracture. He was blind and mute and couldn't move. He had twenty seizures a day. But he lived.

Raymond had a restricted diet and could only tolerate a particular meat-based formula, or MBF, that was manufactured by Gerber. Other, competitive substitutions made Raymond sicker.

But Gerber may not have known this when the company's management decided to discontinue the product in 1985. Demand was low. The formula might have only had a universe of one customer.

The last product made its way through the pipeline and was soon exhausted. Dunn's parents searched the country looking at every Gerber outlet to get the remaining stock.

By 1990, when Raymond was 15, it was all gone. Something had to be done. Without that certain food, starvation would follow. His mother contacted Gerber's management. There were few options.

Gerber was willing to give away its intellectual property to any company that would manufacture for Raymond. But no one was able, available, or willing to take on a new market for a single customer.

It fell to the people of Gerber. They had to do it or the child would die.

And it wasn't the senior managers of Gerber who found the solution. The *Los Angeles Times* reported that it was the employees themselves who became Raymond's internal advocates. They came up with a plan. And sold it to their bosses:

> *Gerber employees who had been working with Mrs. Dunn told their bosses they could assemble the equipment and special ingredients (including beef hearts) to make a limited amount of MBF.*

The company's employees donated time and talent to produce the special product.

Gerber's research director, George Purvis, told the *Los Angeles Times*: "People here are working on this on their own time. We all have our own jobs, and this is one we added on."

A production line was set up. The old equipment was refurbished. Gerber made just enough formula for Raymond—a market of one—and gave it to the Dunns at no charge.

The example Gerber set for their consumers was simple: if a company would do this for one child, how much more would it do for an entire market. This is what effective management looks like.

How can a manager change the world? One tiny market segment at a time.

"Gerber says, 'Babies are our business,' but Raymond's their business, too," said Raymond's mother.

Raymond died at age 20 in 1995. He was known as "The Gerber Boy." And at his death, he still had a year's supply of Gerber-supplied food.

The King will reply, 'Truly I tell you, whatever you did for one of the least of these brothers and sisters of mine, you did for me.' Matthew 25:40

The people and resources of the Gerber Products Company are dedicated to assuring that the company is the world leader in, and advocate for, infant nutrition, care, and development.

The Gerber Mission Statement.

Being effective is different than being efficient, and it takes a different process to achieve. It's harder to measure and harder to direct. In fact, Gerber's decision to help feed Raymond was wildly inefficient. But it illustrates a foundational truth about how effectiveness is rooted in *Completed Staff Work*. A manager's time to think is the most valuable commodity he possesses. And it is finite and in high demand. The number of demands on that commodity are limitless.

The manager's work is never "done." The manager must choose among the infinite possibilities for action in front of him, and *Completed Staff Work* provides the winnowing process that enables his decision-making.

Gerber originally wrote to Mrs. Dunn to tell her that they had no more formula, and no options for making more. It was only through the staff work of Team Gerber—ground-level employees who knew and worked with Mrs. Dunn, who recognized the significance of the moment—that options were generated and surfaced. And leadership listened. *That's* effectiveness.

Peter Drucker writes about becoming more effective in *The Five Most Important Questions You Will Ever Ask About Your Organization* (2008). Companies must be able to answer these five questions, says Drucker:

- What Is Our Mission?
- Who Is Our Customer?
- What Does the Customer Value?
- What Are Our Results?
- What Is Our Plan?

A manager gets graded on organizational effectiveness. Gerber's staff knew their mission and what to do as an advocate for infant care.

The customer is the parent.
The customer value is a healthy child.

An early version of the Gerber mission statement included a section on what the *"Accomplishment of the Mission is Intended to Provide"*:

Healthy-starts in the lives of all children.
Above average returns on the investment of Gerber's long-term shareholders.
And rewarding employment for Gerber associates.

Did extending the short life of one mother's son help with these objectives?
The decision to help Raymond was driven by the employees. And employee satisfaction? By allowing the costly, extravagant gesture, Gerber provided a reward for their employees beyond measure. Commenting on Raymond Dunn, Gerber nutritionist Dr. Sandra Bartholmey said simply, "It seemed like the right thing to do."

Even so, the first job of management is to count the cost, to keep an eye on the bottom line, is it not? How effective was their stewardship of the shareholder's investment? In fact, Gerber was later acquired by Nestle. The company was purchased at a—well, healthy—premium over its share price.

Peter Drucker said that, "Effectiveness is a habit." This is perhaps a reference to Aristotle's *Nicomachean Ethics* where, "these virtues [effectiveness] are formed in man by his doing the actions."

"Doing the actions"—as a habit—day after day. Researching the options, generating a decision tree, presenting The Memo. The good, profitable Effective Organization gets the right things done with military discipline. It's ironic that *Completed Staff Work* originated with the military because it is a formulation of work that empowers employees. This is the opposite of the common misperception of top-down command and control.

The Hollywood version of military discipline stars a tough sergeant barking commands at hapless—powerless—privates who work through rote discipline. However, the reality is dramatically different. The Army's definition of discipline is more, yes, subtle, as follows in two parts:

Prompt obedience to orders, or

The initiation of appropriate action in the absence of orders.

We can all understand that the well-trained soldier or staffer will do as he is told. But the second part is where wars are won and where effectiveness wins, and that is with initiative. *Completed Staff Work* is effective because every member of the team knows what success will look like. Because the manager shared the Commander's Intent. And the team will work toward that common end because the experienced manager will tolerate a minor, or even a not-so-minor failure.

Management lives in the world of imperfection. And by tolerating failure—perhaps, even on occasion, encouraging it—management creates an environment for Initiative. A team of self-starting staffers, encouraged by a manager, will be more effective than the team whose manager only demands compliance and who fears initiative. This staff training is hard work and is the responsibility of the manager.

Drucker continues, "Effectiveness, while capable of being learned, surely cannot be taught." What could he mean by this? This goes back to the hard work of thinking. Evaluating. Making a decision about priorities. Effectiveness is something that is generated through a kind of management alchemy. Effectiveness is the art to Efficiency's science. Becoming effective can only be absorbed through the daily practice of moving systematically with *Completed Staff Work* toward the organization's end goals.

Does your company have too many rules? What is not mandatory is forbidden? What is the Commander's Intent in an Effective Organization? Even large Faith Traditions can get this right.

The story is told of the Jewish rabbi and the Presbyterian minister who were attached with Patton's Third Army as the general's tanks rolled across Europe in WWII. This band of brothers was planning for the worst if they died in their duties. So as was common among the combat clergy, they promised each other a proper burial in the French soil.

Sadly, the rabbi was killed in action within sight of a modest Catholic church. The local priest said that he would care for the remains but that the rabbi could not be buried within the consecrated boundaries of the church graveyard. So according to church tradition, the rabbi was buried just outside the cemetery fence with a proper headstone.

A year later, the Presbyterian Calvinist minister, who had Huguenot blood, returned to the church to visit the grave of his dear clergy-in-arms. He walked around the outside of the fence but could not find the final resting place of his friend. He began to worry.

The French Protestants had warred against the Catholic church dating to the 1500s. The Huguenots believed that the Catholics were obsessed with rituals with the dead and the dying. Protestants, Catholics, and Jews in the region have long memories and were not always allies as they were in the 1940s.

From the rectory, the priest sees the military chaplain and walks over. They instantly recognize each other.

"Where is the rabbi's grave?" asks the minister. "Didn't we bury him on the outside perimeter?"

"*Oui,*" says the priest. "We did. But I felt uneasy having our brave friend sleep alone," pointing to the headstone inside the church grounds.

The minister was confused.

The priest says, "True, there is a rule against burying a non-Catholic inside the grounds." The priest's eyes twinkle, "But there was no rule against moving the fence."

It is not enough to have simple compliance to instructions. Managers cannot and should not give detailed instructions to every employee to cover every possible situation. The good boss does not have too many rules. Competent staff must be trained to exercise "appropriate action in the absence of orders" as the army would say. Staff should be encouraged and trained to exercise wisdom and judgment.

This can be done effectively by inviting the staffer's initiative, within the discipline of the team knowing the mission: What is best for the organization? What does the boss intend? What does the supervisor really need? What does the boss want?

A decade goes by and the local bishop stops by the church to visit with the priest. They take a quiet walk around the church and the silent stones. The bishop pauses by the grave marker with the Star of David and the final year, 1944.

The bishop looks up and into the middle distance.

He walks on, chatting with the village priest…

Effective: accomplishes organizational goals. This is the execution of the assignment where the job is completed. This is Mission Accomplished, Quota Reached, and Numbers Hit. It is the manager's report card. This is where the right things get done.

Discussion Questions
1. What is the purpose of business?
2. How does initiative complement the command's intent?
3. Managers must tolerate some imperfection. Why?
4. Why can't effectiveness be taught?
5. What is the difference between efficient and effective?

CHAPTER 9

Virtue: Staffers do their best work in a state of liberty.

"Only a virtuous people are capable of freedom." Benjamin Franklin

VIRTU IS A CONCEPT USED by Niccolò Machiavelli as a requirement for "the achievement of great things." As the author of *The Prince* and *The Art of War*, (not to be confused with Sun Tzu's book with the same title) Machiavelli's name has come to be synonymous with a kind of ruthlessness that we would not equate with our understanding of virtue.

But Machiavelli believed that his amoral version of *virtu* was required in a leader as a means to grappling with *fortuna*, or "fortune."

"Virtue against rage will take up arms and the battle will be short," he said. Machiavelli would have agreed with John Adams that the leader must control events.

Today we are uncomfortable using a term like "virtue" as a requirement for leadership or effective management. We like to separate virtue from performance. We even deny the necessity for or relevance of such a quality as "virtue."

But perhaps Machiavelli's, let's call it "more martial," understanding of virtue might be easier for managers to relate to. Managers often feel that they are waging a war against rage and fortune. In fact Machiavelli demonstrates that a focus on character as an essential element of leadership should not be characterized as a purely religious, or even merely moral conversation. Virtue in Followership *and* Leadership is a universal concern.

Finding *"virtu"* is another managerial challenge. Everyone wants to work for a manager with good character and all bosses want to hire employees who are trustworthy, harmonious and effective in Getting Things Done. It takes good judgment and virtue to determine the "right things" to do.

"Why on earth did you hire him?" I asked the sales manager. The Senior Territory Manager had shoulder-length hair. He was wearing a leather jacket and a three-day beard that passed for the latest fashion. His eyes followed every woman. He looked like idle Eurotrash sauntering toward a comfortable café to pass the afternoon. Let's call him Rob.

Our work was selling high-end medical devices to hospital accounts. Nurses were the key influencers for our products and services. But these women were more than clients for that one sales representative. They were targets. Rob was a fox in a hen house.

He was a management headache who should not have been hired. Rob's personal appearance was inappropriate for a dance club. His record of poor decision-making and careless work products combined with his attitude, demeanor, and lack of professionalism, made him a disaster in making a presentation intended to inspire trust and confidence in the new medicine we were selling.

John William Gardner, who served as Marine Corps Officer in WWII and later in President Lyndon Johnson's cabinet said, "When hiring key employees, there are only two qualities to look for, judgment and taste. Almost everything else can be bought by the yard."

Rob lacked both good judgment and good taste. He was not "virtuous."

During the job interview, the manager was fooled. Rob was appropriately, conservatively attired and made an outstanding first impression. Con men often do. His hair was short. He was well groomed and sported no facial hair. His suit was conservative and he was well spoken and respectful.

He was on "Vince Lombardi time" for his job interview appointment; that is to say, he was 10 minutes early. His résumé may have had some gaps and there might have been some questions about his performance on the job, but because of the time pressure to fill the position, Rob sailed through the interview process.

So how did he get hired? How, I wondered at the time, could management make such an irresponsible decision? A basic lesson for managers is to ignore expediency where principle is involved. Your Business Professor has learned from experience that instinct often goes hand-in-hand with reason.

Over the decades, I have developed a deep sympathy for the hard decisions managers make. The boss in this example had his reasons to hire this cad.

Staffing a start-up places crushing demands on the hiring manager to find talent in a hurry, and to generate sales *fast* to stay ahead of the burn rate of limited seed capital.

Rob was also highly recommended by his older sibling, who, as one might imagine, strongly suggested hiring his kid-brother, a man-child. Rob's brother, as it happened, was a key customer who was instrumental in our new product launch.

The hiring manager was in a dilemma: take a chance on a job candidate or certainly alienate a significant customer.

It turned out to be a no-win for the manager, as these things often go. And Rob was soon let go.

Wise managers realize as Max De Pree, the former CEO of Herman Miller Furniture and the author of *Leadership Is an Art*, explained,

> *The corporation is an entity only in that it is an expression of each of us as individuals. We know that the soul and spirit, the gifts, the heart and dignity of each of us combine to give the corporation these same qualities.*

In other words, the virtue of each employee has direct impact on the whole corporation. Professor Thomas Dunfee of the Wharton School warns,

> *A company that fails to take steps to produce a climate conducive to positive work-related ethical attitudes may create a vacuum in which employees so predisposed may foster frontier-style, everyone for themselves mentality.*

A smooth major was a brilliant staff officer and a highly decorated combat veteran. He was destined for high command. And his performance deserved it.

But the promotions did not come.

The end began early. At a Christmas party sponsored by his organization, the major danced a little too close with a woman who was not his wife. It became predictable. He did this with different women over the years in public and in private.

His boss noticed. (We all did.) The young guns giggled.

His commanding officer—being a grown-up—was not amused.

The battalion commander gave him promotion-ending efficiency reports. The employee evaluations were open secrets where trust is a matter of life and death.

That warning goes all the way back to the Old Testament where people in trusted positions of responsibility are warned that they have a three-part loyalty test: spouse and family and home.

If, as Benjamin Franklin said, "Only a virtuous people are capable of freedom," then it can also be said, only virtuous staff—made up of people who are honest, trustworthy, hardworking, dependable—are capable of self-management.

If there is a missing link of trust—an employee without virtue—it is not possible to succeed. Team members have to trust one another to complete individual assignments and collaborate on *Completed Staff Work.*

Because of the truth of Benjamin Franklin's observation, the hardest task of a manager is to find the balance between close supervision and empowering employees. That balance is possible only when each individual employee is virtuous. In fact, virtue leads to trust, which enables freedom, which powers effectiveness.

Jack Welch once observed, "If you pick the right people and give them the opportunity to spread their wings . . . you almost don't have to manage them."

Virtue: is where the best people do the best work in *Completed Staff Work.* Virtue is the habit of doing what is right and proper and where there is a fit between the values of the person and organization.

★

Discussion Questions
1. Define virtue and vice.
2. Which virtue is first and why?
3. What is the virtue of accountability?
4. Is it possible to compartmentalize public and private behavior?
5. What is the value of virtuous staff?

CHAPTER 10

Perfection: The individual contributor gets graded on exactness.

PERFECTION IS WHERE THE INDIVIDUAL contributor and organization gets graded against a standard. It means getting the job done without error. It is usually the responsibility of the Individual Contributor, rather than the Individual Manager. It is enough for the staffer to be correct or right in his individual performance. It is not enough for the manager to be "right" in his performance. (See the following chapter on **Imperfection**.)

We are often concerned with our work being perfect. But remember, the bar for "perfection" can be low, especially if you ever worked for Your Business Professor. Perfection can be observed and measured in the individual and in the organization. First, let's examine the big picture in the public domain.

"It's not on the org chart," I said to my assistant as we looked across the document. Since I was speaking as a government bureaucrat this meant that the unit did not exist. My staffer didn't have to study the large hierarchy of boxes and dotted lines that filled the horizontal triple fold-out.

My assistant cleared his throat to get my attention. He was two steps ahead of me, Leading from Behind and all that.

He brought in the Agency Director of the missing department. Even though the manager was standing there, he didn't exist until I (that is, my staffer) found his box in the budget and organizational chart.

It appeared that I had "lost" a $100 million department. It was necessary to find it for obvious political reasons, but we only became aware of the missing unit because I was managing the Year 2000 rollover and we really needed to find all the computer hardware and update the software.

We (that is, my staffer) finally unraveled the problem of the missing department. It was hidden away, quietly chugging along. And there were lots of good explanations why it was floating alone off on its own org chart, in its own universe. How its staff got paid was outside the scope of my narrow search. I was assured that it was not illegal. One learns quickly not to ask too many questions in a very large organization. And, I knew my team would get the precise answers.

The over-performing company is comprised of the actions of perfect individuals who make a team and teams can make smooth-functioning bureaucracies.

Bureaucracy is, "a classical management approach emphasizing a structured, formal network of relationships among specialized positions in the organization." (Bateman, 2012)

Your Business Professor has worked in government, the military, and academia so let us tread softly on how I may, or may not, have attempted large-scale perfection or even added value in various employments.

We should not minimize the efforts of the public employee. As humorist P. J. O'Rourke explains in his 1992 book *Parliament of Whores: A Lone Humorist Attempts to Explain the Entire U.S. Government,*

> *It is a popular delusion that the government wastes vast amounts of money through inefficiency and sloth. Enormous effort and elaborate planning are required to waste this much money.*

Another humorist, Jim Geraghty (or is he a political scientist?), writes on how bureaucracies might self-describe in *The Weed Agency: A Comic Tale of Federal Bureaucracy Without Limits*, 2014,

> *"Where to begin? For starters, how many of our colleagues back in the office would you describe as having great drive and relentless professionalism?*
>
> *Some, no doubt. But a certain portion of those attracted to the public sector's work are looking for ... a different pace than the one demanded elsewhere.*
>
> *A certain stability of eight-hour days leading to a secure retirement, with a certain ... flexibility in quality control. You notice no one ever says, 'close enough for private sector work...'*

Red tape, forms, favoritism, and queues are maligned and blamed for business failures. But where did all this start?

Max Weber was a German sociologist (but of course; from the same country that gave us Bismarck and, well, Hitler) who questioned organizational behavior. He believed that job positions should be based on merit and the competence of the staffer, not on family connections.

He wanted to see results and actual performance so he set up rules. He was attempting to make the workplace fair to everyone, not just to the boss's son. Weber recommended merit-based hiring and promotion. Workmen and skilled craftsmen have always wanted to do perfect work. Weber made it policy.

Let us return to the saga of my missing government agency. My *uber*-competent assistant anticipated the problem, got answers, and found and fixed the missing business unit. The staffer solved the problem and kept me from embarrassment. (Yes, his was a full-time job.)

The staffer was perfect.

Max Weber would have been proud.

★

What is "perfection" in *Completed Staff Work*? It is a flawless product or recommendation that meets or exceeds the standard, the plan, the priority set by the manager. Perfection has microscopic tolerances. It provides answers and anticipates any question the boss might ask.

The staffer's goal is to be the perfect answer-man who delivers on-time and on-budget.

Who is responsible for perfection? The manager sets the expectation and the staffer executes. But perfect followership often requires leadership and initiative.

In the early days of the microblog platform Twitter, its IT staff realized that there was no backup. If the site crashed everything would have be lost. Instead of solving the problem immediately, staffers reported the issue up the chain of command. The manager lost his sense of humor and asked, "…what [insert here your choice of very bad words] are you doing in here?" Instead of fixing the problem, then alerting the boss, the team got it backwards. (Bilton, 2014)

How can staffers get the right action done at the right time? Perfection takes time and thinking. The pursuit of *Completed Staff Work* is a team effort. Options and courses of actions and next steps should be vetted across the organization's multiple points of accountability. You are never alone. Ask for input. Your workspace must never be a solitary confinement.

The Alert Staffer over-communicates, so talk, talk, talk (just not at your boss…).

All this staff working takes a long time to make a short proposal. As the old saying goes, "Cicero excuses himself for having written a long letter, by saying he had not time to make it shorter." Your manager does not have time to read or study a lengthy analysis. You do. Part of the staffer's job is give his manager discretionary time— not to consume this valuable commodity. A recommendation is concise. As the Spanish Jesuit Baltasar Gracian said in the 1600s, "Good things, when short, are twice as good."

What does success and perfection look like without blemish? Supreme Court Justice Potter Stewart once described obscenity as, "I know it when I see it…" *Completed Staff Work* need not be judged by the same measure as pornography. The flawless purity, excellence, and wholeness of the staffer's performance is beauty that can be objectively evaluated. Match the results against the manager's designs and the Commander's Intent.

And finally, *Completed Staff Work* is, well, complete. There is nothing to add. The subordinate should ask himself, "If my manager got promoted, and I was promoted into his slot, would I sign my name to my own recommendation and begin execution?"

Perfection: is the exactness of the work-product of the individual contributor or the company. The staffer is graded on getting as close as possible to a standard or the manager's blueprint. This is Zero Defects, Error-Free, Quality is Job One, or Spotless. It is sufficient for the staffer to be correct, to be right in his individual performance.

Discussion Questions
1. Why is "perfection" the domain of the individual contributor?
2. Explain the phrase, "Close enough for government work."
3. What did Max Weber do?
4. Describe the process to getting a perfect recommendation.
5. How would we know when *Completed Staff Work* is perfect?

CHAPTER 11

Imperfection: The manager is graded on accomplishing organizational goals; being ˣrightˣ is not enough.

THE ONLY WAY A MANAGER can be a superior player is by being less than perfect. A scene from the movie *Martian Child* explains.

John Cusack is mentoring his adopted son, played by Bobby Coleman, at a baseball game and explains the game, life, and indeed, management.

"You know what I love about baseball?" asks Cusack,

> *Baseball is the only sport you can fail 70 percent of the time and still be great.*
>
> *It's about trying hard and never giving up. Just think about it, if you got a hit three out of every ten times, you're really good. If you do a little bit better, maybe 3.2, 3.3 times—you're great and you can be a star.*

A good manager, like a good batter, will be exactly right...about 30 percent of the time. You are not made perfect when made manager.

While individual contributors and normal people are horrified by a 70 percent failure rate, managers nod sagely and say that ".300 is a pretty good batting average." Aspiring managers must understand that there are lots of swings and lots of misses in management. You will not be perfect.

Cusack's character reminds us about the need for persistence and—our favorite buzz-phrase—continuous learning. Baseball players will spend hours practicing the perfect swing of the bat. The batter will do 10,000 practice swings and still fail.

Each player—each business manager—will often strike out and seldom gets on base. Home runs are rare.

Remember: a .300 batting average is a success. A home run can be hit if, and only if, you fearlessly step up to the plate—even after striking out. Top athletes and top managers keep taking—and managing—that risk.

Many new managers are not accustomed to dealing with failure rates, preferring the perfection in their old roles as Individual Contributor. But management, like baseball, does not deal in perfection, let alone in being 'right' with every at-bat. A manager will have a lot of strikeouts even with a perfect, well-executed swing. However, it is all worth it when the occasional ball knocked out of the park brings the crowd to its feet.

The first step to the top of the corporate pyramid is recognizing what the academics, pundits, and other assorted second-guessing armchair quarterbacks do not understand: Management is not perfect. Managers are not perfect. People are not perfect (and managers are people too).

And this is the most difficult challenge that the Individual Contributor must master as he is promoted into management. The work and world of the staffer is getting things exactly right. But the work of the manager is to get things done—through other people. Work must be perfect but people, Lord save us, are not.

When those trouble-employees are not working or killing me with non-performance, then they are dying. In one very large organization, I was attending a funeral once a month. No one told me about this duty in the job description. The dearly departing staffer seldom gave a proper two-week notice of termination.

Machinery can be easy.

People can be impossible.

As the German philosopher Immanuel Kant wrote, "Out of the crooked timber of humanity, no straight thing was ever made." So how does the manager get from point A to B with these imperfect human carbon-based lifeforms?

Relationships. This is the one word that describes management.

Leadership expert John Maxwell teaches us that a manager must nurture his network. This work of interactions starts with the boss, then direct reports, and then internal and external peers. We can only exercise influence and imperfect management through imperfect people.

Imagine a network, a circle surrounding you. If this network supports you, then you cannot fail. If these people-groups of boss, peers, and staffers are apathetic, you cannot succeed. The manager's job is a people-business.

(This is a challenge for Your Business Professor—I am a perfectionist, probably as a result of birth-order. If you don't want to be a perfectionist, then don't be a first-born child.)

Sometimes tolerating some imperfection in staffers is helpful. Here's why. There may not be the budget nor the time to acquire "perfect" employees. Not every employee can be of A-Team caliber. Not every staffer can be made "perfect." Managers can groom and mentor and train but cannot have perfection from all their people all the time. (However, let's not tell the staff this.)

We can best earn their active support by knowing when to tolerate some human imperfections. It's also worth being careful when expecting perfection in a person.

That imperfect staffer may have been touched by an angel.

Literature points us to man's selfish infatuation with perfection and the perfecting of mankind. Nathaniel Hawthorne, who was actually an early science fiction writer, tells a haunting tale in *The Birthmark*, published in 1843.

Hawthorne's story begins with a brilliant man, Aylmer, and his wife Georgiana, a nearly perfect woman. She was exquisite. Georgiana was beautiful and strong and accomplished, and her husband adored her. She was willing to give her life for him.

(Hawthorne is silent here but we can assume that Aylmer would die in her stead also. But he didn't have to.)

Georgiana had a minor blemish, a birthmark on her cheek—a tragic flaw. The mark was faint and delicate as if a cherub patted her cheek. Georgiana's birthmark was all that stood between Aylmer and "perfection." The imperfection at first irritated, soon annoyed, and then hardened the husband's heart into stone. The birthmark needed to be removed for Aylmer's complete happiness.

Now, as it happened, the husband was a scientist and could use his skills to concoct any pill for the betterment of mankind. So our not-so-mad, indeed, very rational scientist retreated to his laboratory and produced a medicinal remedy to "improve" his helpmeet. Georgiana would willingly take it to make him happy.

"Drink, then, thou lofty creature!" exclaimed Aylmer, with fervid admiration. "Thy sensible frame...shall soon be all perfect."

Georgiana drinks the potion, "Methinks it is like water from a heavenly fountain..."

The birthmark began to fade.

"By Heaven! it is well-nigh gone!" said Aylmer to himself, in almost irrepressible ecstasy. "I can scarcely trace it now. Success! Success!"
   "My peerless bride, it is successful! You are perfect!"

Alymer, the scientist got his perfection in the person closest to him. But,

   As the last crimson tint of the birthmark—that sole token of human imperfection—faded from her cheek, the parting breath of the now perfect woman passed into the atmosphere, and her soul, lingering a moment near her husband, took its heavenward flight.

Alymer's work on Georgiana was completed perfectly. But she slept eternally.

Imperfection: is the tolerance of human limitations, which will not stop the accomplishment of organizational goals. The manager must decide how to minimize the weakness of staffers with time, counseling, training, or reassignment. The manager must expect perfection but may not always have time or budget to pursue the flawless, the excellent. Management and people are not perfect.

Discussion Questions
   1. Why is management a practice in imperfection?
   2. How is managing like a baseball at-bat?
   3. Explain the crooked timber of the human condition.
   4. When can imperfection not be tolerated?
   5. What is the management lesson of *The Birthmark*?

CHAPTER 12

Benefit: ˣWhatˣs in it for Me (and the organization)?ˣ

WHY DO WE DO WHAT we do? The leader and follower should always understand the root cause of a person's motivation. This helps the relationship for the manager to accept staff recommendations getting *Completed Staff Work*.

Why do you care?

Why?

"I desperately need a job and will say anything to get on anyone's payroll."

That's not exactly what the job supplicant said, as he lay prostrate begging in front of my desk. But it's what was communicated.

This was not what I wanted to hear—because I was the desperate one. I was anxious about getting the slot filled so my team didn't have to take on the work of a missing person. I didn't need to see desperation in others.

I was looking for talent. I wanted someone with smarts to save me from myself—to prevent or rescue me from my own actions. Yes, I have an eternal Savior who has taken on my sins. But I was also in search of another kind of savior, so to speak, to protect me from my own stupid decisions.

This requirement is vital for every manager, but is never listed on the Knowledge, Skills, and Abilities checklist. I must know why the candidate is motivated (so I can harness this drive to move my agenda). Advancing the organizational goals would be a plus.

So the interview continued as they all do. The candidate tells me what school he attended, his GPA, activities, what-this, what-that.

Whatever.

If we didn't run out of time, then maybe I'd get some of the "how." How he came to Big University, how he'd earned that GPA, how he'd come to join Big Fraternity, and how he'd performed his duties. How'd-duty.

Nice and conventional. But I needed to learn more if I was going to select the right candidate for the right position. And I was getting bored. So I asked the job applicant to tell me a story of a problem he overcame.

But I didn't give enough direction to my would-be storyteller. What I really wanted to know was the "why" he did what he did.

I should have started my job interviewing the same way the late Steve Jobs, founder of Apple, did. "Why do you want to work here?" Steve Jobs would ask. "Why?"

After he understood the individual's motivation, then he got to the "how" and finally to the "what."

Steve Jobs was moving through a "why-how-what" template. I did the reverse in a "what-how-why" manner. Jobs assuredly made better hires than Your Business Professor.

We now understand the why-how-what better through the work of Simon Sinek. Born in England, Sinek teaches at Columbia University in the city of New York, and runs a consulting firm focused on getting to everyone's "why."

Simon Sinek says, "If you hire people just because they can do a job, they'll work for your money. But if you hire people who believe what you believe, they'll work for you with blood and sweat and tears."

We want staff who will put their hearts and souls into the work and we want to avoid those who labor only for money. As Scripture warns in Matthew 15:8, *These people honor me with their lips, but their hearts are far from me.*

In 1979, CBS reporter Roger Mudd interviewed multimillionaire Ted Kennedy, senator from Massachusetts. Mudd asked a simple question, "Why do you want to be president?" Kennedy could not answer. Roger Mudd later described Kennedy's response as "incoherent and repetitive" and "vague, unprepared." His response can still be watched on YouTube as the singular moment of when his campaign crashed before take-off.

He could not answer the "why" he wanted the job. His heart wasn't in it. Or maybe he was desperate.

Our story continues in another job interview. The job applicant was overqualified. He was exactly what our team needed.

He was living in boisterous New York City, but was now sitting in a job interview with me in quiet Richmond, Virginia. He was applying for a state government job with a four-year term. We would be lucky to get him.

He was an outstanding match to the job description. His experience fit our needs. He loved our work and the team loved him. It would be a win-win and all that. He was perfect. But.

But something was not adding up. What was in it for him?

Why should I trust you? Why do you want this job? Why should I do business with you? It is not enough to tell me how fabulous you or your product is. I want to know why you are driven. There is always a reason why. Find it in yourself and tell me.

What is "inside" that works to help those "outside?" Why do you work? Don't tell me that you "love people." My dog loves people. Give me the reason. Our deepest motivation provides the compelling reason we do what we do. "Follow your passion?" Sure. But tell me why.

Let us look deeper to other possible origins. The reasoning of why we are motivated can be explained through:

Trauma
Young memory
Mentor's guidance

In trauma we recognize and remember pain. We avoid it for ourselves and should help others avoid similar agonies. Your Business Professor has committed countless errors and this propels him to help others avoid such misery. It is an attempt to salvage some good for others from "my bad" as the young might say. "I was there…" makes for a compelling witness to explain motivation.

Our young memories drive our behavior. Picture the momma duck with her baby ducklings following behind her. She's bigger, more experienced, and wants to protect her young. "My daddy always said…" is a good way to explain why you are so inclined. It is easy to understand motivation when a person points to childhood experience and its accountability throughout life. Imprinting can be understood just as a duckling will follow his larger mother for food and safety.

It is cliché to speak of your third-grade math teacher who sparked your interest in finance. But it is the believable bridge that moves you and explains your position today. It also telegraphs to the hiring manager that you are coachable and grateful.

★

My gut was bothering me about that perfect job applicant. Something was missing from his curriculum vitae. I needed to know the why of why he was sitting in front of me. I asked him, "Why on earth would you leave The Big Apple for the small potatoes of the Confederacy's capital?"

The job applicant got still and lowered his eyes. He raised his head and said that both his parents were ill and he needed to be close by with his extended kin and the family's large land interests. "It is," he said, "time to come home."

Now I knew his "why." He was hired and served the organization well. The "why" matters.

Benefit: is the advantage to staffer and to the manager and to the organization. The managers' work is to identify talent, those who are self-starters driven by self-interest. Managers must know how to lead and motivate and match the desires of the staffer and needs of the organization.

Discussion Questions
1. Can money buy happiness? Or loyalty?
2. Why do teams need coachable players?
3. Is WIIFM (what's in it for me?) selfish?
4. Hiring managers look for symmetry. Why?
5. A staffer should also interview the manager. Explain.

CHAPTER 13

Trust: This increases the staffer's value to the manager.

TRUST SPEEDS DECISIONS AND INCREASES the staffer's importance to the manager.

Trust is earned by the manager and the staffer and is not quickly fast-forwarded. It is a faith in a current condition and hope in the future. Trust is confidence that the staffer's suggestions will be honest, reliable, and effective.

> *I am sending you out like sheep among wolves. Therefore be as shrewd as snakes and as innocent as doves. Matthew 10:16*

Gaining trust is elusive and is the result of leadership and followership. This mutual assurance depends on the manager, the staffer, and the situation. Why is trust necessary? What happens without trust? And finally, how can we create trust?

Why is trust needed in *Completed Staff Work?*

Nobel laureate Milton Friedman spoke to this problem. He said that a cultural prerequisite of making money efficiently is the holding of truthfulness as a common virtue. "It cuts down transaction costs," says Friedman, "when you can trust a merchant's word." And trust the customer. This saves time and time is, well, money.

Organizations are downstream from culture. Confidence in good character and integrity between manager and follower promotes efficiency to speed decision-making and resource allocation.

Remember, the manager does not have time to do all of the thinking or consider all of the options to make a decision. Reliable, able and honest staffers can assure the manager that a particular recommendation has the lowest risk.

What does the lack of trust look like in the practice of management?

A trustless organization can be a terrible place to work. Decisions will be made slowly, if at all. Staff work will be incomplete because the chief is less likely to accept anything submitted. "If you want something done right, you gotta do it yourself..." is the mantra of the amateur manager. So the entire organization locks up waiting for the manager to do or decide.

And when this inexperienced supervisor does manage, it is at the micro level. Micromanagement occurs when the boss is forever watching employees' every move and not allowing the staffers to make a decision.

Micromanagement is caused by:

1. The manager is inexperienced and /or
2. The staffer is inexperienced and/or
3. The situation is high risk.

The manager who has yet to learn the science, art and practice of management will reserve all decisions, large and small, for himself. Learning to delegate is hard work. This is the inverse of *Completed Staff Work*. Peter Drucker wrote in *The Effective Executive*:

The Definitive Guide to Getting the Right Things Done, "An executive who makes many decisions is both lazy and ineffectual." (Drucker 2006)

The staffer might also not know what he's doing and require close supervision. But this should only be a temporary necessity and not a permanent condition.

Finally, the state of affairs might be so novel or risky that the manager should be "hands-on" and closely monitor the critical situation. This should be rare. If it is not, then different staff and management is needed.

Even the biggest organizations, and the most celebrated CEOs, have challenges trusting their teams. Marissa Mayer, president and CEO of Yahoo!, has been reported to be "… a micromanager in the extreme…" In fact, one biographer reported that "Mayer spent as much time on Yahoo's parking policies as she did strategizing over the billions of dollars Yahoo! would net from its final sale of Alibaba stock." (Carlson 2015)

"Just give me a chance," says the exasperated staffer. We are talking about his authoritarian manager. "He just doesn't trust me."

"How long have you been here working for him?" I ask.

"All week…"

Trust is best forged over time and can seldom be rushed. Developing trust is subject to a simple formula:

The bond of trust requires a track record and accountability — both of which take an investment of time.

Proverbs 25:15a advises the subordinate, *Through patience a ruler can be persuaded…* A track-record of performance is not established overnight. And there is no substitute that provides authentic managerial confidence. The fear all managers share is that the confidence is rushed, misplaced and might damage the organization. Mastering *Completed Staff Work* can provide a foundation for building that trust because volunteering for tasks can benefit the organization; it is not selfish.

★

The terrorists commandeered the plane and took hostages. An elite FBI negotiation team was called in and within a few days the hostages were released. How does this happen?

This was the timeline of hostage negotiation seen in any number of instances over the decades.

Q: How did the good guys influence the hostage-takers?

A: A small step at a time.

Here's what it might look like. Communication is set up between the terrorists and the negotiators and a relationship is established. Both sides talk. Demands are made and considered. Time passes and the terrorist, crew, and passengers are getting hungry. A (discrete) number of Chick-Fil-A sandwiches are delivered to the plane.

The negotiators ask for the plastic trays back.

If the terrorists give the trays back, it will be only a short period of time before the hostages will be released.

The negotiators don't care about the silly plastic trays. What they were doing was getting the terrorists to move in a microscopic step in the direction of accepting the influence of the authorities. The small reasonable steps of getting "unreasonable" terrorists to submit is an art-form of persuasion we can practice in an even more dangerous venue.

Like, for example, your office.

Let's say you (the subordinate) need something only your manager can do.

The boss doesn't have time, you do.

But he has the authority, you don't.

You have time, but no authority.

Ask your supervisor for a small-tiny-infinitesimal favor, which will cost him nothing. It will require no time to ponder your meager request and no effort to grant. You should appear to be under no time pressure. It is an odd condition of management behavior that you will be appreciated more by the boss when the boss helps you. *Noblesse Oblige.*

In time ask for a slightly larger favor. In time, do this again.

These negotiation techniques are so effective that terrorists now don't bother with hostages anymore and use aircraft for other weaponized purposes.

Trust: increases the staffer's value to the manager. Trust is earned by the manager and the staffer and is not quickly forwarded. It is a current condition in a future hope. Trust is faith in the staffer's suggestions—that his recommendations can be adopted. Trust shares a Hebrew root in "truth."

Discussion Questions

1. How is trust efficient?
2. How can trust increase a person's value?
3. Describe micromanagement.
4. Trust is earned in small steps. Explain.

CHAPTER 14

Process: Appreciate the work and the numbers will follow.

MY DAUGHTER HANNAH WAS BEING recruited by a coach with a track record of consecutive championships. I wondered how he won so consistently. I asked her to ask him, "What was the one thing he looked for in putting together a team?"

The coach said, "Athletes who love to train."

He wanted, as do all managers, staffers who are internally motivated and love the work of the organization. Self-driven people are easier to lead and to motivate. All that's left of the manager's work is to plan, organize, and control.

The coach/manager can then:

- decide the course of actions (plan—what to do)
- choose which resources are required (organize—who to do)
- evaluate the outcome back to the plan (control—how did it do)

If the manager provides the resources and the staffer does the work, the results will follow. It sounds simple but often is not.

My cell phone bill was $1,800. It was the 1980s and business was learning the benefits of the new technology. I loved the immediate follow-up and improved service. We were seeing efficiencies gained with continuous communication for the traveling salesman: me. But I was paralyzed when I got the bill. "This is awful," I said to John, my sales manager. "My sales don't cover my salary or—this month—even my expenses." We were part of a thinly capitalized start-up with slow revenue growth.

"True," John says. "But your job is to generate the sales. Place the product in the customer's hands and we'll figure out profitability soon enough."

★

The boss was right: establish the relationship (my job) and good management (his job) would give the product a future. It was a team effort.

My manager had played collegiate football and knew well the link between coaching in sports and managing in business. Indeed, "Coaching *is* management," says Dr. Jerry Bell, founder and CEO of the Bell Leadership Institute and professor at the University of North Carolina. (Bell 2004)

The University of North Carolina's legendary basketball coach Dean Smith talked about his coaching philosophy—the process that led him to the Basketball Hall of Fame,

We asked our players to concern themselves with things within their control, our mission statement was: Play hard; play smart; play together. We knew if we did those things, we would be successful a large percentage of the time. (Bell 2004)

A game's final score and a business's profit are merely the byproducts of the end results of well executed behaviors. The daily drills, work, and workouts are the processes that move us incrementally to our goal (line). Keeping a focus on process—the blocking and tackling of management—is how supervisors do their job.

The cell phone was expensive. However, I did not understand at the time the "organize" part of management. This is the decision of the manager to select the people, budget, and the resources to do the job. My sales manager's encouragement was part of the "lead" definition. The "control" part of management was the evaluation of my sales numbers. And that was the source of my worry. I needed to fear less about the cell phone cost and do the work. This was my appointed task.

My sales manager promised that I would get all the resources that I would need to do the daily drills to reach my sales goals. Just as commentator George Will once wrote, "If you will an end, you must will the means to that end."

My boss paid the $1,800 cell phone bill.

It matters not the labor; we must love the work, whether competing in sports or launching a new product.

Or building the atomic bomb.

Robert Oppenheimer, who led the Manhattan Project, is known as the "the father of the atomic bomb". Historian Ray Monk writes,

> In the early part of the 1900s most physicists, "worked on a problem in order to solve it; Oppenheimer took pleasure in the work itself." Italics in original (Monk 2013)

Quite simply, Oppenheimer loved to train. He loved the process. Dr. Oppenheimer found and recruited fellow scientists who loved the work of physics as much as he did. A British scientist said that he managed Los Alamos, the city/university/laboratory/factory as a philosopher-king, "the most exclusive club in the world...I found a spirit of Athens, of Plato, of an Ideal republic." (Monk 2013)

Before a manager can join his team on the mountaintop of Olympus, he will need to plan the building-block behaviors to get the organization off the ground.

I was walking all day and getting nowhere. My assigned goal was to sell one vacuum cleaner each day. Impossible, I thought. The product was frightfully expensive, appealing to the tiniest of market segments and the appliance was sold going door-to-door. I didn't know what I needed to do (which was odd, since I was then a teenager, I knew everything...).

My sales manager and trainer, George, noted that I had the skills, attitude, and behaviors, but I was desperate to get that One Sale Every Day. I was doing the right things right. I enjoyed helping families delight in healthy and clean carpeting. But I was always missing my goal by half. George then explained the sales funnel.

Our company had extensive research to determine the steps to get one sale:

- For every 100 doors knocked upon, 3 families would agree to a lengthy product demonstration.
- For every 3 face-to-face presentations, 1 would result in a sale.

I now understood the process: Bang on 100 doors and no matter what the outcome for any one door, 100 knocks would get one sale. It was the law of the large numbers and the right behaviors. Process got results where enthusiasm had failed me.

The manager and follower cannot manage the result—the outcome and the numbers. We can manage the behavior and the process to produce the numbers. The plan part of management is to determine the activities the team should complete. The numbers should follow.

So I doubled my input and the numbers instantly flowed down the funnel. At first this was a chore, but then the work produced the numbers, just like George predicted. One sale a day made my day and made my manager happy and made me money. I learned to love the process.

I was lucky. We had data that could help guide my manager with his planning. But the manager may not always know what behaviors will create a customer and make a profit. The boss may need a recommendation on what to do. And this is the action in *Completed Staff Work*—secure the research on the process that will motivate his team to get the numbers.

Process is the action step taken by staff which will result in measurable performance. Profit and an organization's effectiveness are outcomes from behaviors. This is the work where the best managers design daily tasks in incremental, easily digestible portions so that the team can accumulate small frequent victories to the larger goal.

Discussion Questions

1. Numbers cannot be managed, only behaviors can. Explain.
2. Why are self-motivated employees easier to manage?
3. Can the knowledge worker be managed? Explain.

4. Describe a manager's plan.
5. Must all plans originate from the manager? Explain.
6. What is a sales funnel?
7. Describe process and profit.

PART THREE:

Path: How to Manage
Completed Staff Work

CHAPTER 15

Indecision: Stop the dithering, boss.

I know your deeds, that you are neither cold nor hot. I wish you were either one or the other! Revelation 3:15

THIS BIBLE VERSE COULD HAVE been written by any number of frustrated subordinates. Managers get paid to decide. They get paid to decide to "not-decide."

They do not get paid for indecision.

What's the difference?

The manager needs to answer, *when does debate stop and the execution begin?*

Your subordinates are pushing back. This is what you want; you didn't hire yes-persons who polish apples. You need a real debate to get the best recommendations to help you make the best decision. You want a heated discussion around the conference table, sometimes even with pushing and shoving.

The best bosses demand vigorous deliberation to vet a course of action. No unthinking rubber-stampers are on your team, right?

But sometimes the push-back pushes the manager over the edge. When is debate too much? How does a staffer understand when to stop debating and start executing?

The manager and staffers should know as a matter of policy when the debate turns from a dialogue of equals to the hierarchy of superior and subordinate. When the manager with authority decides then the followership of the staff begins.

The debate is over when the manager has made the decision.

The Alert Staffer can determine this by asking the manager a simple question, "Is the debate over and has the decision been made?" If the answer is yes, the arguing arm wrestling is over, and then the execution begins.

Talented managers make decisions and are, well, decisive. There should be no doubt further down the org chart that the talking is done and action is to begin.

However, if the staff does not know that the decision has (really!) been made, then confusion, the push-back, pleading, and whining continue.

We have an example of a time when even the Creator of the universe was reconsidering a decision.

Abraham, a good man, is arguing with God against destroying Sodom and Gomorrah. First, he asked for God to spare the city if 50 righteous men could be found. God granted his request. Then he asked for 40. Then 30. Abraham just kept lobbying God. Finally [Abraham] *said, "May the Lord not be angry, but let me speak just once more. What if only ten* [righteous] *can be found there?" He answered, "For the sake of ten, I will not destroy it."* Genesis 18:32.

Those ten could not be found. And the destruction decision was to be carried out. But Abraham's recommendation was partially granted whereby his nephew Lot and his family were able to escape.

Managers must make clear the bright line that divides debate from decision. When the boss has signaled that the line has been crossed and the decision has been made, then the debating and second-guessing is over.

The Planning and Organizing is over. Leading the Execution is about to begin.

The manager can decide to not make a decision and alert the staff. When faced with an unusual conundrum or high-risk choice, a decision maker might make the deliberate move to develop more information or options. This is making a decision. But this action must be balanced with team motivation and timeliness.

Thirteenth century philosopher Rabbi Maimonides said, "The risk of a wrong decision is preferable to the terror of indecision."

Sometimes a decision is made to postpone or to make no decision. "Louis XIV was a man of very few words.... His infamous 'I shall see' was one of several extremely short phrases that he would apply to all manner of requests." (Greene 1998).

But most of the time the chief is concerned—let us not say "worried"—about making a decision because not all the data is available. Everyone would like to have complete and perfect information. But time will never allow that.

Secretary of State and four-star General Colin Powell wrote, "When you enter the range of 40 to 70 percent of all available information, think about making your decision. Above all, never wait too long, never run out of time." (Powell 2012)

And finally, an example where incomplete staff work meets a decisive decision maker.

Be Brief, Be Brilliant, Be Gone, goes the cliché—the subordinate must be clear with definitive recommendations.

My father lived because Niels Bohr couldn't do this. Thank God.

My dad was a teen at the end of WWII and would probably have been part of the invasion of Japan, code-named Operation Downfall. The Allied strategy was to win the war first by concentrating on the defeat of Germany, then Japan. After VE Day (Victory in Europe), our attention turned fully to the Japanese empire.

We had a secret, terrible weapon to end the war fast. But there were scientists who did not think we should drop the bomb.

Niels Bohr visited President Roosevelt in August 1944 to persuade him not to use the atomic bomb, which was being developed as a weapon and said that the technology should be shared with the world. Bohr talked too much, and said too little too late. It took him 30 minutes to get to the point of his argument.

No CEO and no president has time for that kind of throat-clearing wind-up. Historian William Manchester wrote, "Roosevelt disagreed with Bohr and bade him good day." (Manchester 1973)

FDR was decisive. Bohr was not.

It is not likely that Bohr could have persuaded the president not to drop the bomb in any scenario. But he did not deliver the best presentation for that point of view.

The staffer can persuade his manager in less time when the relationship has been nurtured. The boss can more quickly adopt the advice of a subordinate when the staffer communicates efficiently and effectively.

The staffer must package the information and the recommendation as a marketing exercise to promote the product to fit the desires of the decision maker. The recommender can use shortcuts where a common language has been developed over time.

But here's how the boss really makes a speedy decision. When he,

> *Trusts your ability,*
> *Likes you, and*
> *Appreciates your integrity*

Competency in presentation skills can be learned. General George Marshall, when he served at the Infantry School, insisted that student officers practice delivering short, simple orders orally— standing up. General Marshall was teaching a new generation of Army officers to think fast, reason well, and to speak plainly on their feet. (Ricks 2012)

Historians report that during WWII General William Hood Simpson was a delight to work for; he was known for issuing orders in such a manner and early enough to allow for proper planning, what would be commonly known as a warning order. This gave subordinate units time to begin to get ready. Not every detail was necessary to begin to move in the correct direction. The fleshed-out final orders would follow. (Ricks 2012)

And this is not just for words but also for figures. "For any presentation or talk, you'll be wise to observe…the three Rs of numbers: Reduce, Round, and Relate," wrote James C. Humes, speechwriter to five presidents. (Humes 2002)

This simplicity can help keep your manager from indecision. Remember: a confused mind always says, "no."

President Theodore Roosevelt said, "In any moment of decision…The worst thing you can do is nothing."

★

Niels Bohr did not prepare properly to learn how to best sell to President Roosevelt; he didn't know how FDR processed information.

Roosevelt died in April 1945. Vice President Harry Truman assumed office and continued the strategic use of the atomic weapon. Truman was decisive. He dropped the bombs on Japan on August 6 and August 9. Japan surrendered unconditionally on August 15, 1945.

Dad came home and finished high school.

Indecision: Manage the manager to make the cut and stick with it. No decision has been made? The experienced staffer helps move the manager away from foggy confusion. A memo can be used like a contract. It can be a signed document: vetted before signing and widely disseminated after. The red-line, qualifying question is, "Has the decision been made?" If no decision has been reached, then we can continue the debate. If the decision has been reached, then we can move to execution.

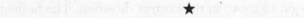

Discussion Questions
1. How does management indecision hurt motivation?
2. What is the difference between deciding not to act and indecision?
3. When does the debating stop and execution begin?
4. Will the manager ever have all the information needed? Explain.
5. *Completed Staff Work* moves decisions faster under what three conditions?

CHAPTER 16

Promotion: Move to greater authority.

Robert Eichelberger, Walter Krueger, Oscar Griswold, Alexander Patch.

George Patton, John Foster Dulles, Omar Bradley, Spaatz.

The first group is nearly unknown, unheralded. The second group has nearly household names.

What is the difference?

The first group was led by General Douglas MacArthur, and forgotten. The second group was led by General Dwight Eisenhower, and venerated.

General Douglas MacArthur was a military genius. He personally is well known and his life story is enshrined and studied. But there were some flaws. His senior subordinates are all but unknown today. He did not elevate or promote his team in the press or share the limelight of success.

Newspapers of the day knew only of the greatness of MacArthur when his team succeeded. The only time the media knew the names of his subordinates was when there were setbacks. MacArthur took glory in victory and evaded responsibility in defeat.

When the subordinate British commander Field Marshal Bernard Law Montgomery was getting too much favorable press during the Normandy invasion in WWII, President Roosevelt had to direct the Supreme Commander Eisenhower to take more action to get more attention. Shared glory made more for all.

Promote your subordinates to get promoted.

Genuine leadership prepares subordinates for future responsibilities. This has at least three benefits:

a) The organization can continue to thrive in any absence of the leader.

b) Morale of staff can be improved, as employees know they are being trained and developed.

c) The manager is easily promoted where there is trained staff to fill vacancies.

The manager is easily promoted where there is trained staff to fill vacancies.

This is the anticipation in *Completed Staff Work*. The best manager must train deputies who can take over on an instant's notice, if for no other reason so that the manager can travel away from his office or maybe even take a vacation. "Hands-free management" will train the subordinate for more responsibility with little risk. Absence can make the heart fonder and the team has the opportunity to demonstrate competence

This should also teach the manager to go "hands-off" and not be tempted to micromanage the manager in training. The trainee should practice without fear of getting fired, even if he doesn't get promoted.

Dean Acheson, President Harry S Truman's Secretary of State from 1949 to 1953, offered advice to develop leaders,

There are only two things we can do. One is the way we've operated since the Spanish-American War, which is to trust the commander in the field, say to him, "Go to it, brother." You don't say, "Send this division here, or use these supplies and movements there." Churchill tried to do that and got everything bollixed up.

The second way is to relieve him—and who wants to do that?"

Dan Pink, former speechwriter to Vice President Al Gore, writes that we each want to get better in what we do. We want to learn more. We want mastery. Even if a business does not have a formal "Office of Staff Development" in the Human Resources department, a good boss will encourage the continuing formal and informal education of his team.

The manager might as well cheer the training—his people are doing it anyway, and taking classes even if there is no credit or recognition. Millions are absorbing nondegree, electronic-learning from Massive Open Online Courses (MOOCs) like Kahn Academy, the cutting-edge online math tutoring website, to sharpen skills.

Succession management planning and training has benefits to the company, the team, but the real benefit—dare we say—is for the manager herself. The easiest person to promote is the manager who has her replacement trained, in the chain of command and who is eager to assume more responsibility immediately as the boss moves up the corporate ladder.

And the manager cannot do it all himself anyway. He must train and commission deputies to share the work load.

How does the manager groom leaders? Using "Safe Failure." Should the manager rejoice in a trial by fire?

Pattie was a good hire and I encouraged her manager to move her up to bigger projects. Assignments with greater responsibility, budget, exposure, and risk. Even though she was going through the pain of growing, her supervisor was quietly making the wager and taking the risk and betting on her.

Her performance was not a sure thing. Real growth requires bending and sacrifice and concern. To give Pattie "a chance to grow" she was placed in progressively challenging assignments. Sometimes it was painful to watch. (Yes, it hurt me more than it hurt her...)

Our current age believes that progress can come without stress. Growth needs tension and perhaps trauma.

The New World Orderlies of our current age believe that a sustainable, friction-free environment can be manufactured. They tried it in the Arizona desert. This "Utopia" was not pretty.

It was called the Biosphere and was all the rage from 1980s to the early 1990s. Hippie turned Harvard MBA John Allen wanted to eliminate external randomness in life and replace our "dead civilization...and press on to build a more acceptable and satisfactory future." Biosphere was a self-sustaining environment in a closed container—a shrinkwrapped geodesic dome built for some $200 million. The Dream World didn't come cheap.

The "scientific" Biosphere attempted to eliminate the unknowns and ban any ugly intrusion of the Uncontrolled, Polluted, and Overpopulated Outside. They wanted to create a perfect, tranquil environment without the normal messiness of mankind.

That is what did the killing.

The fish died. The cockroaches were fruitful and multiplied.

John Allen and nine Biospherians attempted to control variables, eliminate climate change in a risk-free zone in an enclosed manmade (very large) recycling bin. They lived for two years without direct outside contact.

It was a Skinner-like three-acre terrarium protecting the insiders from outside contamination. They wore stylish jumpsuits by Marilyn Monroe's fashion designer.

A rare case where style didn't help.

This Bio-Utopian project ended in a *Lord of the Flies*-like management meltdown between competing factions on strategic direction. They stole food and squabbled over money. Imagine.

But we did (re)learn at least one fact of life: stresslessness, like weightlessness, is not always best. The hermetically sealed Biosphere produced weak, unhealthy, saggy trees. There was no wind, no real breeze in the bubble. No wind meant no movement of the trees. No tree movement meant no "exercise." With no buffeting winds to bend the trees the plants became weak. Even an ill-wind would have helped.

Both plants and people need challenging head winds to become strong creatures. The Biospherians wanted to eliminate variables and vulgarities and ended up with sick trees, dead insects, and starved

The student of *Completed Staff Work* looks for and expects troubles on this earth. Indeed, we should rejoice in our trials. Preacher and professor Randy Yeager, Ph.D. writes,

We are even happy when trials beset our path...because we have learned that tribulation generates patience which, in turn, generates experience which, in its turn generates more hope..." (Yeager 1983)

Now, Dr. Yeager is lecturing on eternal salvation that will follow earthy trials. He just as well could be writing on promotion on earth.

★

Queen Fredericka, a character in Mark Helprin's *Freddy and Fredericka*, says, "I wake up in the morning and pray for difficulties—not small ones, not ringing someone up to have him change a light bulb, but the difficulties that, by counter-pressure, enliven the soul." (Helprin 2005)

Let us return to Pattie. Your Business Professor, back in his managing days, gave assignments (re: extra work) to develop team members and to learn who could face a challenge and deliver results. Most staffers, it seemed, were content in their job description and current station. These staffers would politely, respectfully beg-off, citing other responsibilities.

Pattie stepped up, sometimes stumbled, but kept asking for even more assignments (that extra work stuff). Her every bruising decision and skinned knee made her stronger for the next opportunity. She battled for promotion and earned it.

Peter Dawkins was a West Point graduate and a Rhodes scholar and the Heisman Trophy winner in 1958. [1] In the early 1960s he wrote in *Infantry* magazine,

> *The ideal almost seems to be the man who had done so little—who has exerted such a paltry amount of initiative and imagination—that he never has done anything wrong...*
> *The was a time when an individual wasn't considered a very attractive candidate for promotion unless he had one or two scars on his record...*

---

[1] General Dawkins, Ph.D., earned a general's star and became Vice Chairman of the Citigroup Private Bank. His life was blessed but not easy. Dawkins had polio as a child.

If [a man] is to pursue a bold and vigorous path rather than one of conformity and acquiescence, he will sometimes err. (Rieks 2012)

★

Relax—there is work to be done and must be done right, but what is the right work?

You are the CEO deciding between two candidates for a top management position.

One manager is brilliant and hard-working.

The other is brilliant and, well, lazy.

Which manager do you pick to get things done? The hard-working supervisor.

Or that lazy one?

Is this even a decision?

Yes.

But odds are you picked and promoted the wrong guy. You went for the very busy over the not-so-busy. And you would be fooled. By a busybody.

Definition: The professional manager gets things done through the thinking support of others. Too much of the "work" that most managers are doing should not be done by the manager. It is true, as Proverbs 14:23 says, *All hard work brings a profit, but mere talk leads only to poverty*. But what is "work" for the manager?

The manager's job is to plan, organize, lead, and control. In contrast, the individual contributor does the doing—the hands-on work.

The amateur manager confuses what his work is and what it is not. Your Business Professor made this mistake both as a young Army officer and as a new manager. I was hard-working and brilliant. (Citation source: the author's mother).

But I wasn't very smart. I was doing the wrong work for a manager. I was doing too much of the doing and not much of the delegating. I was doing the tasks of an individual contributor and not much of the work of a manager.

Your (Teutonic) Business Professor can be rather direct and harsh in using "lazy" as a description. Richard Koch, a writer and former manager at Boston Consulting Group and partner at Bain and Company, offers a better word. He suggests "relaxed" rather than "lazy." (Koch 1999)

The manager's job is to see that the work gets done—through others. And not to do the work themselves.

When the "relaxed" manager understands what his work is, he can then be effective and advance the organization's goals, create a customer, and bring in a profit. Picking the right team and making a good hire is the hard work of profitable management.

Promotion: is the move to a greater position of authority by showing competence in your current position and in the confidence of superiors. Genuine leadership is not barking out orders and demanding instant obedience. Amateur managers believe in the simple loud, vertical master/servant positioning. But building horizontal relationships and coalitions inside and outside the organization are essential abilities for successful leadership.

Discussion Questions
1. What is the advantage to grooming a successor? 112-18
2. Can the amateur manager safely take a vacation? 112
3. What happens to trees without winds or storms?
4. President Roosevelt had polio. How does pain promote?
5. The individual contributor should work too much. Not the manager. Explain. 117
6. Why are scars attractive?
7. Will a mistake stop a promotion?

CHAPTER 17

Narrative: Storytelling is a skill; parables make for good leadership and followership.

GENERAL GEORGE MARSHALL KNEW HIS country and countrymen well. He was bringing men who were drafted into the army during World War II and was molding them into a cohesive organization with a will to win.

The country in the early 1940s was divided about its international involvement. Not all draftees were excited about serving. They came from different ideologies and backgrounds and regions. And the American male is not a compliant creature.

How did Marshall move them?

Marshall insisted that the young men, and their mothers, who loaned them to their country, sending them toward battle, have the war explained to them. He knew that the nation could not be dictated to or lectured at—American mothers and fathers would have to be persuaded with a compelling argument.

So was fulfilled what was spoken through the prophet:
"I will open my mouth in parables..." Matthew 13:35a

Who did Marshall enlist, so to say, to sell the war?

Not Jesus.

Hollywood.

Frank Capra, who actually did enlist in the Army, offered his services. Capra was already known for his direction of the Academy Award-winning movie *Mr. Smith Goes to Washington* in 1939. Wearing an army uniform, Capra directed a series of seven films on *Why We Fight* commissioned by the U.S. government to educate the Army's recruits. Disney did the animation of the maps.

It is often said that we live today in the sight and sound generation. But images, especially those that move with an audio accompaniment, are most convincing in any age. *Why We Fight* was important.

General Marshall put Capra in an office near his own. A Colonel explained to the creative genius,

> *You were the answer to the General's prayer... You see, Frank, this idea about films to explain "Why" the boys are in uniform is General Marshall's own baby, and he wants the nursery right next to his Chief of Staff's office... (Capra 1971)*

Leaders will use the tools of persuasion and must know what they are, and what they are not. Management has four well-known principle parts: plan, organize, lead, and control. The benefit of *Competed Staff Work* is the selling of a recommendation, whether it comes from the employee or from the chief.

The verb "to lead" is thought by some to be the command component of managing, where orders are barked out and then instantly obeyed by compliant subordinates.

This is a fantasy. And Marshall knew it. This is what made Capra's storytelling work vital to the war effort.

The Frank Capra films were broadcast in the medium of the day, movie theaters, to a nation hungry for news. The influence and magic of the motion picture industry rallied the nation to war. The first film, *Prelude to War*, earned an Academy Award in 1943 from the Academy of Motion Picture Arts and Sciences for Best Documentary film.

General Marshall understood the American soldier of the 1940s just as outstanding managers understand the company employee of today's generation. The individual contributor, a soldier with a weapon, or the carpenter with nail gun, or knowledge worker on a keyboard, is each motivated in the same way. They, indeed all of us, are stimulated best *not* when externally coerced by outside pressures, but when internally driven to deliver. Marshall and Capra captured this internal drive and motivated millions in *Why We Fight*.

Today's manager best exercises influence by creating his own *Why We Work* for his own people, by telling a story.

Every leader is a storyteller and knows the value of the vignette.

"What's the story?" is commonly asked by the elite consultants at McKinsey & Company. The question helps the firm to develop world-class recommendations for clients. Here's how it works.

Every problem or opportunity can be condensed, explained, and understood in a short narrative. We should use a short tale because,

> *A parable is a specific story that has broad applications.*
> *The arc of the narrative, the story line, is simple to tell and remember.*
> *The story focuses attention.*

Jesus used parables to teach eternal lessons. This question can also help in the hiring process.

The job interview is a sales presentation where we match the candidate's experience to the needs of the organization. But the match-up is seldom perfect. The new person in the new position will face challenges that the hiring manager may or may not know, but he must be confident that the job applicant has the potential to excel.

The narrative can persuade the hiring manager that the candidate's past experience provides a transferable skill to the new organization. All story lines have three simple parts divided into a three-act play.

Act I is the Problem. Act II is the Solution. Act III is the Result. In every job interview, Your Business Professor will ask, "Give me a short example of a problem you faced, a solution you devised, and the result of your initiative."

Here is one of my favorite responses from a job seeker,

> *I was working at a 7-11 as a cashier.*
> *When faced with a sudden snowstorm, [Problem]*
> *I contacted my cousin who has a snowplow on his truck and we cleared the parking lot so that customers could get to the store [Solution].*
> *This provided customer safety and increased the store's daily sales— triple the same-day revenue from the previous year [Result].*

What manager would not hire this applicant for almost any position in his organization? The storyline helps the manager to remember and concentrates attention and next moves on getting this kind of initiative onto his team.

Will storytelling always work? Maybe not. Even Jesus had trouble with his disciples. They were sometimes slow to grasp the expanded meanings of his short stories. Mark 4:13 says, *Then Jesus said to them, "Don't you understand this parable? How then will you understand any parable?* How did Jesus help them to comprehend his instructions?

With another parable—and with repetition.

So follow Christ's example and have at least one vignette to tell your story and your organization's story.

Tell a story that has this three-act play, Problem, Solution, Result. The Alert Reader will note that Your Business Professor often says, "I am the luckiest guy on the planet." What's that all about?

At a recent funeral (they seem to come faster and faster as we get older and older) my wife Charmaine and I talked about burials.

Charmaine asked what we'd do with the ashes, where on earth to put them. "Where do you want to be buried?" she asks, expecting I will say the family's burial plot.

"37°18'N, 137°55'E," I say.

"What?"

"The Sea of Japan," I remind her. She just looks at me confused, getting impatient. (She's normally good with numbers.)

"What's there?" she demands.

Bonefish.

The young Torpedo Man carried his sea bag onto the war-bound submarine *USS Bonefish*. He never left.

During World War II, my dad skipped out of high school and followed his older brother into the Navy. He was assigned to the sub that is, even now, on "eternal patrol" as the Silent Service would say.

It was a random assignment that took my dad off the boat and put another man aboard.

★

A manager gets things done through communicating with other people. Roger C. Schank, a cognitive scientist, tells us how to do this best, "Humans are not ideally set up to understand logic; they are ideally set up to understand stories." (Pink 2005)

Indeed, says TED talker Dr. Brené Brown, "Stories are data with a soul."

Christ spoke of life-changing principles in parables. Simple stories can be re-told and remembered after the boss has left the building. Every story should have a theme, a plot divided into three parts: the Conflict (Problem), the Struggle (Solution), and the Happy Ending (Result).

Act I introduces and develops the characters and brings out a conflict of the protagonist.

Near what was to be the end of the war, to speed the end of the war, submarines were dispatched to the Sea of Japan to destroy what little enemy shipping was left. But the war, as we now know with hindsight, would be over in August. Did the navy have to still need to be so aggressive?

But at the time the navy's leadership did not know how soon the war would end. So risks were measured and taken, and *Bonefish* was caught and sunk by the Japanese.

That lowercased-brand writer, ee cummings, remarked that there are no second acts in America. But this is misunderstood in a life's drama. Act II reveals the agony of the possible decisions and outcomes.

In our current times, we are too impatient to deal with the middle act, the part of the drama where there is way too much time-consuming character development and confrontation.

ee cummings didn't mean that there were no second chances or that there were no "comebacks" from failure. Indeed, the American culture is a story of come from behind... of redemption... of looking to the future.

Dore Schary, who wrote the script to the Oscar-winning movie *Boys Town*, said to Harvard Club LA, "America is a happy-ending nation." (Manchester 1973) The best tales present the characters living happily ever after—where all's well that ends well, riding off into the sunset.

If you're buried at sea, there are no headstones. We cannot mark the grave of the man who took my father's place, so we mark the date. We pay silent homage in remembrance of June 18, 1945, when the sea smashed through the bulkheads and turned a warship into a coffin.

A half-century later, after fighting in and surviving two wars, my father was buried in Arlington National Cemetery. He had the chance to raise a family and devote thirty years to the armed services, and pin second lieutenant bars on my shoulders.

He didn't talk much about the *Bonefish* or the man who replaced him.

Still, I imagine in some Navy Valhalla my dad and this other sailor linked up together and asked the Creator, "Why?"

"Why him? Why me?"

Why was my father not on that submarine that fateful day?

And the answer does not come. Only that my father's grandchildren now live. With a purpose and a destiny still unknown.

Act III has the resolution of the conflict to The Happy Ending.

The only stories that work, the only stories with impact; the only stories that spread are the "I can't believe that!" stories. These are the stories that aren't just repeatable: these are the stories that demand to be repeated. (Godin 2009)

The submariners' association members sat with skeptical, blank faces. They thought Your Business Professor was going to give the typical politician's speech: a pandering, colorless, suck-up to the Greatest Generation (as I would normally deliver).

Instead, I told the story of "why" I was grateful: sailors changing places, the kith and kin in the back row.

At the end, a small prop aircraft flew over our small gathering and headed out to sea. A wreath was dropped near the horizon to remember the submariners lost at sea, still on eternal patrol.

My dad lived and I was born, so my children are here to fulfill a purpose larger than themselves. They have a debt of honor to pay to that young torpedoman who took my dad's berth, and where he sleeps still.

Writer Gail Godwin describes teaching and selling as the transference of emotion and says, "Good teaching is one-fourth preparation and three-fourths theater." (Godwin 2014)

Michael Novak, the philosopher novelist and diplomat, wrote, "Americans wish to believe that their leaders control events. The fact is that the chief role of leadership is that of symbolic reassurance. Leaders need not do anything. But they need to give the appearance of hard at work, on top of events, and in control. (Novak 1970)

The practiced leader tells a story.

John Wesley Yoest walked off the doomed boat, survived the war, married his high school sweetheart, and she had me. I have a duty to that young submariner who took my father's place. I am grateful.

Narrative is a storytelling skill. A short vignette can help sell an idea. A story can persuade the staffer's manager to adopt a recommendation. Or can help the leader sell a vision. The arc of a narrative follows the template of defining a problem, recommending a solution and describing the result. The storyline can instruct the "why" of why we do what we are doing.

Discussion Questions
1. How is storytelling a part of *Completed Staff Work?*
2. Describe the three acts of a play.
3. How can a story be data with a soul?
4. How is a story spread?
5. Why did Jesus speak in parables?
6. Why is a Happy Ending necessary?
7. What's your story?

CHAPTER 18

Alliances: Find friends to sell the boss.

IT WAS A SUNDAY. COUSIN David was driving a new Lincoln out of state and bending the speedometer needle hurrying home. His passenger was The Judge. They were stopped by the friendly state police and issued a citation with a required court appearance the next morning.

David didn't mind the fine but he couldn't show up in court because he had to be at his construction business early Monday as he had concrete to pour. But it was the weekend and all official offices were closed.

What to do?

The Judge says, "Stop at the next town; we gotta *find a friend*."

So they stopped at the local State Farm insurance office on Main Street, made introductions to the agent on duty, and told him their dilemma. They discovered mutual friends—six degrees of separation and all that.

The insurance agent knew the jurisdiction's law enforcement (his brother, I believe) and invited his kinfolk over. David confessed, paid the fine, got back on the road, and headed home with The Judge.

In trouble? Need to sell the boss on an idea? Remember that you are not alone; no man is an island as John Donne reminds us. Yes, we must face Our Maker alone as we cross over to eternity, but we should not face anything alone on this side. We all need support at one time or another. Or all the time.

The Air Force calls this relationship a Wing Man; the Army has the Ranger Buddy; the Navy a shipmate; the civilian counterpart has "got your back." Scripture calls this "a friend."

If one falls down, his friend can help him up. But pity the man who falls and has no one to help him up! Ecclesiastes 4:10.

Find a Friend.

Completed Staff Work is teamwork. We've been talking about managerial decision-making as a process of getting to "yes." But more often, the manager's job is to say "no." As Peter Drucker reminds us, a manager's job is to use *Completed Staff Work* as a winnowing process to produce the best decisions:

This means...

> *That management's most important power is the veto power, and its most important role is to say no to proposals and ideas that are not completely thought through and worked out.*
>
> *This concept is caricatured in that well-known jingle composed many years ago by a senior Unilever executive.*

> *Along this tree*
> *From root to crown*
> *Ideas flow up*
> *And vetoes down. (Drucker 2013)*

The professional staffer we discussed in Chapter 7, Followership, knows that a manager will accept a "completely thought through" proposal when it has had the benefit of multiple sources of input and has the support of the team. He wants to see proposals that have been vetted. In most large organizations, the manager also needs to see that coalitions have been formed and attention paid to the internal and external political cost. Make it easy for your manager to endorse your recommendation; let him know the extensive political support your proposal has.

How does the Alert Staffer build this backing? With a network.

Do not forsake your friend...Proverbs 27:10a

"You should always go to other peoples' funerals; otherwise, they won't come to yours." Yogi Berra had it, well, almost right. The great Yogi Berra is said to be the best catcher in baseball history. The Hall of Famer played almost two decades for the New York Yankees. He was a beloved manager who mangled quotes and created enduring friendships.

The catcher on a baseball team is traditionally perceived as the most intelligent player on the field—the one who gets things done.

Yogi loved the game (winning) and loved people (who did the winning). He understood the subtle movement and magnetism of how people behaved like family on a molecular level. Leaders and Followers understand these relationships and how to get people to get things done.

Management is done through the thinking support of others. Management described in one word would be "relationships."

Inexperienced managers think that the work of the manager, that plan-organize-lead-control, is what is done "to" subordinates beneath them on the org chart. The novice leader thinks that 100 percent of his effectiveness depends on getting his direct reports to work.

This is, of course, wrong. To "control events" the manager needs to control more than the workings of his staff. Where does the new manager begin?

He can start with some new business math.

The manager's world has four bodies in his orbit. His boss and his staff above and below on the vertical; his external peers and internal peers on the horizontal. They each have to be maintained in balance.

If we simply allocated equal time to each group of relationships in each of the four quadrants we would see 25 percent of the manager's time working with his internal peers, 25 percent of his time nurturing relationships with his peers outside the company, 25 percent with his boss's office, and the remaining 25 percent with his staff.

Most of the manager's time should be invested, not with his people, but apart from his direct reports.

This is also true for the individual contributor who is managing his own career and projects. We all need support even outside the orbit of our immediate management. Each follower must invest resources to build coalitions to be in place to sell a suggestion to the manager.

The mature manager and follower understand that the directions of who helps who can be reversed and interlocking.

Thomas J. Watson, the senior, chairman and CEO of International Business Machines (IBM) said, "A manager is an *assistant* to his men." To be an effective staff assistant the professional, seasoned manager knows that his people don't need a hands-on assistant handing them tools. The staff has needs that only the manager can provide.

I once asked a commanding general his greatest challenge in running a large organization. He said, "to put resources where my people need them—or me…My office is BWI airport." He traveled extensively to meet his team in person and get them what they needed to get the job done.

The experienced manager knows office politics and movement of political capital and the extended relationships that govern them.

CEO, entrepreneur, and former Air Force officer Erik Larson reminds both managers and staff in *A Checklist for Making Faster, Better Decisions* in *Harvard Business Review* to, "Involve a team of at least two but no more than six stakeholders. Getting more perspectives reduces your bias and increases buy-in…"

Can *Completed Staff Work* be done without the log-rolling backscratching of office politics?

No.

Robert Greene writes in his 1998 bestseller *The 48 Laws of Power* that,

> *If the world is like a giant scheming court and we are trapped inside it, there is no use in trying to opt out of the game. That will only render you powerless, and powerlessness will make you miserable.*

What does building alliances look like and how does this help in *Completed Staff Work?*

Coalition: The mathematics that every leader masters.

Consultants Tom Peters and Robert Waterman, Jr. tell us how this work in building alliances begins *In Search of Excellence* (1982),

> *Leadership is many things. It is patient, usually boring coalition building. It is the purposeful seeding of cabals that one hopes will result in the appropriate ferment in the bowels of the organization.*
>
> *It's building a loyal team at the top that speaks more or less with one voice.*

All politics, whether office or elective, works on the power of simple arithmetic: addition and multiplication, not subtraction or division.

Management Professor Henry Mintzberg reminds us that the best managers seldom "solve" anything—they settle. He quotes Chester Barnard in the classic 1938 work *The Functions of the Executive*, "It is precisely the function of the executive . . . to reconcile conflicting forces, instincts, interests, conditions, positions and ideals."

Managing Mintzberg writes, "Notice [Barnard's] use of the word reconcile, not resolve." (Mintzberg 2009)

Barnard's work in management and in organizational behavior taught us that the reconciling starts inside the organization.

If the leader cannot manage inside the company, he probably will not be able to manage outside, between organizations. The real professional takes this talent uniting factions inside the company and on to aligning interests outside the company.

Does the alliance building mean that values must be compromised?

No. Taking a small, incremental step in the direction of one's goal is usually how agenda's are advanced. "Three yards and a cloud of dust..." as Ohio State football coach Woody Hayes said.

How can the Leader get input? Through the grapevine.

In the days of sailing ships, fresh drinking water or other fluids were transported in barrels called "butts." A hole would be drilled or cut into the container to allow access to the liquid. The casks or barrels were known as "scuttlebutts" where the crew would gather.

The business counterpart today is the office water cooler where "rumor control" is centered. "Scuttlebutt" is the seagoing term for rumor or gossip, while "grapevine" originated with the Army. Nautical meets landline.

Jitendra Mishra, Ph.D., Professor of Management at Grand Valley State University,

Allendale, Michigan, writes,

> The term grapevine can be traced to Civil War days when vinelike telegraph wires were strung from tree to tree across battlefields and used by Army Intelligence. (Kreitner 1983)

The messages that came over these lines were often so confusing or inaccurate that soon any conjecture was said to come "from the grapevine." Today, informal lines of communication seem to be haphazard and easily disrupted as were the old telegraph wires. However, the grapevine transmits information rapidly and in many cases faster and with a stronger impact than a formal system allows.

Official lines of communication and the flow of information are well documented in meetings and memos and the content is slower to change.

But the company grapevine is a casual, natural communication network outside the solid lines of the company org chart and works at the speed of moving electrons. The office grapevine is the fastest conduit for any number of tidings, good or bad, and has remarkable accuracy.

The manager can control the grapevine with about as much effectiveness as controlling human emotion or office romances. The boss must be "in the loop" for one dominant reason: he must not be surprised. The manager may not always be able to "control" the content of the grapevine gossip, but leadership must know what it is—to "plan, organize, and lead" recognizing the rumors and working with them.

The American Management Association reports that a grapevine commands attention because the network is right about 80 percent of the time. This might be more accurate than the authorized interoffice memos.

Professional managers know to monitor the office gossip.

Former Secretary of State Colin Powell said, "I treasure the person who sees opportunity before anyone else and smells risks and threats early." (Powell 2012)

Alliances: are formed in finding friends/co-workers/stakeholders to help sell an idea to the boss. The manager will have greater confidence if a number of his direct reports and influencers back a plan. This reduces risk. There is safety in numbers (of allies).

Discussion Questions
1. Of what value is to *find a Friend?*
2. Why do managers say "no" so much?
3. Who is on the manager's orbit?
4. Managing is addressing conundrums. Explain.
5. How is the manager the assistant to his staff?
6. What is the grapevine?
7. How does the leader/follower build alliances?

CHAPTER 19

Debate: The best leaders need candor.

"DO YOU CONSIDER US SYCOPHANTS?" Decimus Brutus asked Julius Caesar.

That provoked a laugh. "No! Sycophants don't lead legions capably, my friend...*My* legates aren't afraid to tell me when I'm wrong."

Colleen McCullough writes of leadership and followership and of managing debate in her 1997 book *Caesar, A Novel*. In capturing the genius of the Roman Emperor, she writes, "*No man functions at his best without opposition.*"

Caesar inspired fear—and feedback?

When is "backtalk" effective? Can a respectful employee give honest advice?

"We could do that," said one of my direct reports, a key senior supervisor. "But it wouldn't be right..."

It was a direct confrontation delivered ever so softly by a follower skilled in leadership. He would do this when I was about to go in some random direction. I would make a blundering move, occasionally (OK, maybe not so occasionally). And he'd be ready with a course correction suggestion.

I would be swerving like a drunken driver and he would guide me back to the straight and narrow.

He was such a pain in the backside.

I didn't know how lucky a manager I was.

★

In World War II, General Albert Coady Wedemeyer, was a key aide to the Army Chief of Staff George Marshall. As the story goes, he ended up in one exchange arguing heatedly with Winston Churchill. Historian Mosley reports that Marshall approved:

> *Afterward, [Wedemeyer] had apologized to Marshall for having talked back to such a distinguished statesman... "Wedemeyer," he had said, "don't you ever fail to give me the benefit of your thinking and your knowledge and experience." (Mosley 1982).*

And if you cannot give feedback then quit the position. Former Secretary of Defense Donald Rumsfeld advises, "Be able to resign. It will improve your value to the President and do wonders for your performance." (Rumsfeld 2013)

Because the mature manager will regret not resigning—when the times demand it.

Army Chief of Staff Harold K. Johnson knew that President Lyndon B. Johnson was leading the country the wrong direction during the Vietnam War. General H. K. Johnson said that he had decided to resign, but vacillated. He explained,

> *...then on the way to the White House, I thought better of it and thought I could do more working within the system than I could by*

getting out...And now I will go to my death with that lapse in moral courage (Ricks 2012).

This is the Virtue Gap—the gap between the right decision and the action actually taken. The greater the difference between what should be done and what is done, the greater the unhappiness. The good general knew the right course of action. But he took a course of action miles apart from the appropriate path.

General Johnson was plagued by the gulf. Candor takes courage. He lacked both.

He suffered.

The country suffered.

Contrary: the mature manager nurtures dissent?

The leadership got it wrong in the Great War and then got it wrong in the Great War Redux. The failure was not listening and learning.

Charles de Gaulle (1890 to 1970), president of France from 1959 to 1969, had the gift of governance. A tall man at 6 feet 5 inches, he looked over the heads of others and had vision to see over the horizon. He proved prescient in understanding evolving events and technologies.

But that was yet to come when he wrote *The Army of the Future* as a young lieutenant colonel in the 1930s. Like Patton, he understood that static defensive lines seen in the trenches of World War I would be bypassed by fast-moving motorized equipment.

Charles de Gaulle said, "The machine controls our destiny."

He was right.

These would be German war machines.

After World War I, the French learned the lesson that a static defensive line was nearly impossible to breach. France built an impregnable position along the Franco-German border, the Maginot Line.

Charles de Gaulle, however, argued that static defenses were obsolete in modern mobile warfare. He stood alone; his younger voice was ignored by decision makers.

In World War II, France was overrun in the German blitzkrieg, The Lightning War. Hitler's motorized army simply maneuvered around the impregnable Maginot Line on the northern flank by going through neutral Belgium.

France fell in a month in 1940.

And so, de Gaulle was a voice in the wilderness about the lessons to be learned from World War I. The start of WWII could have been different if the counsel of the future president of France had been adopted.

What do you say about yourself?" He said, "I am A VOICE OF ONE CRYING IN THE WILDERNESS..." John 1:19-23

In business, war, and politics, effective managers must make decisions based on available options and recommendations. The best managers are thinking two moves down the chessboard of their field of play. Few tasks are harder than staffing backup plans, a Plan B, anticipating change.

German Field Marshal Helmuth Karl Bernhard Graf von Moltke (the Elder) (1800 to 1891) wrote, "No plan of operations extends with certainty beyond the first encounter with the enemy's main strength."

This is translated from German. The translation into English can better fit a bumper sticker, "No plan survives first contact with the enemy."

Or as boxer Mike Tyson once said in so many words, *Everyone has a plan until you punch them in the face. Then they don't have a plan anymore.*

Stuff can go wrong and disaster can come from any direction. My old sales manager once said, "There are a thousand ways you can get bit in the [backside]."

Moltke (the Elder) was the forerunner to Murphy (the Laws) as we learned in the Vietnam War management. Professor Andrea Gabor at Baruch College/CUNY writes,

> *To technologists and managers, the end of WWII marked a clear triumph of both American technology and managerial methods... (Gabor 2000)*

If good management—*Completed Staff Work*—won the Second World War, then bad management lost Vietnam.

Robert McNamara was Secretary of Defense advising Lyndon Johnson on the war in Southeast Asia,

> *What was missing, acknowledges McNamara, was debate. "I clearly erred by not forcing—then or later, in Saigon or in Washington—a knock-down-drag-out debate over the loose assumptions, unasked questions, and thin analyses underlying our military strategy in Vietnam. (Gabor 2000) (McNamara 1999)*

He did not have discretionary management time, or a stand-up deputy, I would venture. McNamara did not get or did not demand *Completed Staff Work.*

McNamara didn't get good recommendations and had nothing good to sell LBJ. What does it take to persuade and to win?

> *It requires the highest degree of self-discipline on the part of managers and willingness to take upward responsibility to keep higher management, and especially the corporate top management, informed, knowledgeable, and educated. It also requires the "executive secretariat" or "business research staff." (Drucker 1973)*

Find that contrary voice on your team to dig out the real numbers; usable research. He might see something you don't. (Gergen 2001)

What device can a manager use to get staff reactions; second opinions?

★

The 360 Degree Evaluation is pattern recognition and a feedback tool in monitoring people performance.

In this century, Germany has given us World War I, World War II, and the Multisource Assessment, a multi-rater feedback...

The German Army used this as an evaluation instrument for their Officer Corps in WWII. (Wikipedia 2014)

Germany lost World War II, of course, but this control element lives on in every American organization. Human Resource Managers now call it the 360 Degree Evaluation.

This instrument is a measurement of personnel effectiveness. A 360 Evaluation gets input from those evaluators who encircle the target or—rather—the employee. The person in the center is graded by his boss and also by staff who report to him. Internal and external peers complete the review. The evaluation is usually anonymous except for the appraisal from the boss.

The 360 Evaluation works best with Commitment, Confidentiality, and Candor.

The boss, boss 2, boss 3, and boss [to infinity] must be committed to getting feedback from all sources. The management team must actively support the concept of being in the center of accountability. The manager does this by submitting to the same humiliation of the nameless backstabbing as endured by the rest of the company. No one is exempt.

The 360 Evaluation works only in guaranteed, anonymous privacy. Your Business Professor once had a manager who inadvertently disclosed the name of one of my direct reports who had made a number of petty criticisms of my superior management style. I was able to rise above the malcontent's snark. *Noblesse oblige* and all that. But our relationship (which is the one word that describes management) was tainted. That was because from that day until that complaining subordinate left, I hated his guts.

(Yes, yes, I am working on that Christian charity character component...)

A 360 Evaluation works when the boss is behind it and the staffer is nameless; this should encourage direct, honest opinions. These days Your Business Professor even does a 360-type evaluation in which my students get to grade me. The critiques are usually helpful.

In the absence of any special form from HR, you might consider the following format to get feedback from your circle of tormentors,

To improve the effectiveness of this organization, the manager [that would be you] should,

Keep doing this:

Stop doing this:

Start doing this:

I also ask for a numerical grade based on a 100-point scale, and advice to raise my score.

The real value of the 360 Evaluation is to encourage the organization and stakeholders to communicate with management. Managers often get complaints from customers and our employees. Perhaps not every criticism is valid.

But what managers should be looking for is a pattern of behavior where company values are being violated. The boss must act on a repetition of a complaint from multiple sources. The pattern is what is important.

General Ridgway, who kept the Free World from losing the entire Korean peninsula in the early 1950s, reminds the manager that he must control events or be controlled by them. But he must know what the events are. He cannot be in the dark.

Ridgway said, "The only inexcusable offense in a commanding officer is to be surprised."

President George Washington warned a commanding army general, "Beware of a surprise! I repeat it: Beware of a surprise..." (Hogeland 2017)

How does our modern manager learn to anticipate events and to not be surprised? What does he need?

Candor.

Candor is defined as an unreserved, honest, or sincere expression; forthrightness. However, candor's first definition is "whiteness, brilliance." The Latin-related roots include candid and the Old English "candel." From these origins we get "candor" and "candle." We get the light, which dispels the darkness.

How does The Thinking Manager get candor in his life? He asks for it. Nonstop. Perhaps no one did this better than the Irish Catholic congressman from Massachusetts, Thomas P. "Tip" O'Neill. He served from the early 1950s to the late 1980s. He is best known for the maxim, "All politics is local." He died in 1994.

Tip O'Neill loved to talk and as he walked the halls of Congress, he would greet every passerby. He worked the local office politics. He would ask everyone, "What do you hear? What's new? What should I know about...?" He might start every meeting by quizzing his staff to get information on all the congressional members (let's not call it gossip). He was seldom surprised. He knew everything about everybody. He was elected by his peers to be the Speaker of the House from 1977 to 1987. (O'Neill 1987)

★

Another popular politician during this period, Ed Koch, also invited—no, demanded—candor from his constituents. Mayor Koch would accost New Yorkers on the subway and from every street corner, with, "HowmIdoin?" (How am I doing?). He'd get an earful. They loved him. He served as NYC's mayor from 1978 to 1989.

The best managers are never surprised by events.

★

Inflection Point: how does the staffer know when the debating is over?

There is a limit to candor.

"All I get is push-back; nonstop yammering and foot-dragging," the CEO said.

"Foot-dragging...?" I asked. Presenting questions is what consultants do when we can't figure out what the heck is going on.

"Yes," said the Big Boss. "They call it 'analysis' but all they do is run their mouths and I'm trying to run a company—"

I still don't know what was going on. Time for more stupid questions, "You hired those guys for their wisdom and experience, and when you get advice you complain?"

"I didn't hire them; I inherited them." The Boss is angry. "I should have cleared out that deadwood when I took the job..."

He has lost me. I was trying to find out what direction he was headed with his three problem-causing senior vice presidents so that I can get in front of him and give him what he wants. (I know where my bread gets buttered.)

I asked, "What are we trying to do? Are we having an employee evaluation for termination or an execution discussion?"

The CEO looked down and considered. He is respected for being known as an enlightened liberal leader (in the traditional definition) who empowers his staff. But now he is impatient. He will fire or lose 10 percent of his team this year but he cannot replace all of his SVPs at once, as appealing as it might be.

"No," he said. "I just want them to do what I—we—have decided."

I knew the three SVPs in question. Maybe not the brightest bulbs in the marquee, but they were not entirely incompetent. They can follow clear instructions. They could—probably—pour water out of a boot as long as the CEO put the directions on the heel.

I said, "Yes, but we do want their input…" I use the second-person plural sounding officious and smug like a psychiatrist or an academic or maybe a nurse, *how are we feeling today?*

"No, I don't."

"What?" I remain lost.

The CEO was mad at them and was getting mad at me, "No," he said, "I don't want a continuing debate after I—we—have made a decision. I—the decision has been made—and now I want some work done around here."

And so I learned a lesson from my client. This happens a lot. A strange business, consulting. I learn something and then submit an invoice and get paid for it. Odd.

I now understand that Getting Things Done comes in two stages: Talk and Action. (Years, yes, *years*, of advanced study is on display here.) Cut bait or fish. Candor is nonstop but there are times when debate ceases.

CEOs and managers want creativity and discussion and vigorous, direct advice in the recommendation phase. They then want to move to phase two: compliance, movement, and doing.

Careful: This is office politics and diplomacy. Candor, out of phase, with bad timing, might sound too much like second-guessing and whining.

★

Evil: What happens when numbers rule and debate does not?

I was lucky; I was driving a Pinto that didn't kill me. Long ago Your Business Professor regularly drove a friend's Ford compact from the 1970s.

He bought it cheap.

I would have known why he got it at such a fire-sale price if I had been aware of all the deaths caused by exploding gas tanks in rear-end collisions. It was never hit, and I was lucky.

The Pinto crisis was a man-caused disaster. It was not caused by driving. But it was reckless homicide. Was it money and profit that bedeviled Ford's leadership?

Maybe not.

Money is not the root of all evil; it is the *love* of money that is the root of evil. It's important to make the distinction here because a good businessman loves to make his numbers. But sometimes that love turns deadly.

In the late 1970s Lee Iacocca was the president of the Ford Motor Company and tasked his team to compete in the small car market. He said the new car should cost less than $2,000 and weigh less than 2,000 pounds.

The Pinto would be brought to market in a lightning-fast twenty-five months instead of the usual forty-three. The engineers would kill to make those numbers.

What could go wrong? Critics write that the,

> *Exploding Pintos caused at least fifty-nine deaths and, as a result, gave Ford the dubious distinction of becoming the first U.S. carmaker ever to be charged with reckless homicide. (Gabor 2000)*

But can we blame the automaker? Ford had missed the zeitgeist, the spirit of the times. The public had become safety conscious above all else as compared to an earlier time in automotive history where,

In the late forties and early fifties...Ford introduced cars with seat belts. But sales dropped catastrophically.

The company had to withdraw the cars with seat belts and abandoned the whole idea.

When, fifteen years later, the American driving public became safety-conscious, the car manufacturers were sharply attacked for their "total lack of concern with safety" and for being "merchants of death." (Drucker 1973)

Ford's error and the ignored fix was highlighted in the courts during the trial,

Since the price of avoiding burn accidents ($137 million) was nearly triple the benefit of doing so ($49.5 million), the company never authorized the change. (Gabor 2000)

Joan Magretta, former editor at *Harvard Business Review*, wrote that Ford's efficiency-driven Pinto beancounters did "...careful calculations of the benefits—all the costs associated with those burned and killed down to the flowers at the funeral...Cost-benefit analysis said it just didn't pay to redesign the Pinto." (2012)

This is where a focus on ruthless efficiency undermined effectiveness. Ford lost sight of its safety mission. Perhaps more internal debate would have brought this problem to the surface. Indeed, candor between staff and management can be a lifesaving best-business practice.

Debate: is demanded by the best leaders. The boss needs candor, diplomatically delivered. Every initiative must be vetted and have a devil's advocate in opposition. The push-back debater is often seen in the child-like audacity of a court jester who is unafraid to confront the "Emperor with No Clothes."

★

Discussion Questions
1. Why didn't Caesar like sycophants?
2. One should be able to resign. Why?
3. Debate and candor take courage. Explain.
4. How could the Ford tragedy have been avoided?
5. How can surprise be avoided?
6. Do 360 Degree Evaluations help managers? How?
7. How do diplomacy and candor work together?

CHAPTER 20

Execute: Implement the manager's decision.

THE PURPOSE OF MILITARY COMMAND—OR any command—is victory *and* getting things done.

He wore a private's uniform with only general's shoulder straps. The president of the United States promoted him to rank of Lieutenant General in command of all Union troops against the Confederate Army.

Why did Lincoln promote the unassuming Ulysses S Grant to lead in the dark days of 1864?

"He fights."

Lincoln's short answer communicated that the behavior "fights" would produce the outcome "victory." The beleaguered president needed a commanding military leader who would keep fighting until he won.

Careful planning is the first part of the description of management—plan, organize, lead, and control. Planning exercises are beloved by academics and consultants. However, the complaint from the end-users is that all plans have assumptions and are machine-like, even robotic.

The chin-stroking consultants (we) dream it up. They've done their job and then heave the heavy books with their 12-point plans and 10 appendices down the hall into the manager's office. The hapless boss is then charged with producing real-world measurable results.

Planning documents sometimes make dangerous assumptions. Resources will be on-hand when and where they are needed. Competent staff will be able, available, and willing.

And that the execution will be flawless.

Except when it isn't.

Which is always.

Because after the planning is done, it will have to be executed. This is the organizing (who) and the leading (how) parts of management.

Early in the Civil War, Lincoln was frustrated with his key army general. General George B. McClellan was elegant and loved by his well-groomed, Northern, parade-ground troops. His planning documents, when he produced any, were also elegant. His plans were beautiful and complicated—and too clever by half.

The overly cautious McClellan never got anything done. There was lots of movement, but no victory.

Lincoln finally replaced showy McClellan in late 1862. Fancy plans and fancy pants were not enough if the work didn't get done.

Lincoln tired of sophisticated planning documents (and would have even if they had been downloadable using a convenient app). He needed something done. Lincoln and the Union needed a soldier-general with muddy boots who pressed the battle.

Enter Ulysses S Grant. Rumpled and rough—he didn't stop until he won.

The Matrix: one vision, one goal, one boss ensures success.

Your Business Professor has reported to many managers over the decades. And usually, like most staffers, I had only one boss at a time. But once as an entry-level, empty-headed, blank slate, I was assigned to report to two supervisors at the same time.

Big mistake.

I usually upset my superiors one manager at a time, but having two supervisors enabled me to goof-up twice as fast.

Assignments came twice as fast while my incompetence grew exponentially. I was hardly able to follow the direction and vision of one boss, let alone two. I was confused on my own; trying to please one boss was hard enough.

In my youth and inexperience, I didn't know that I had been set up for failure—inserted into a matrix organization where one person has a dual reporting relationship. One staffer with two managers is a recipe for disaster.

I didn't like it.

Scripture doesn't care for it either. Matthew 6:24 says, *No one can serve two masters. Either you will hate the one and love the other, or you will be devoted to the one and despise the other...*

My experience actually went beyond the biblical. I think both managers hated me. And I didn't care much for either of them either.

A matrix organization is much like the movie of the same name: The Matrix. To execute a complicated story-plan, it needs exceptional talent. And that wasn't me.

A matrix can work with some high-end consulting firms or high-technology, medicine, or academia. This is where we might see really smart people in a temporary team, for a defined project, with a clear end point. It might work.

But for most companies, a singular vision directed through a traditional pyramid chart still remains the best and most manageable template.

Duplication: there is one sure path to mission success.

The Alert Reader will remember my dilemma from Chapter 5. "You have the assignment?" I said to the guy running legal. "I thought I had the assignment." I was running human resources.

We both were given the same task by our mutual Big Boss VP who was layers above us on the organizational pyramid.

We only found out about the dual delegation when we began dueling for resources to do the job. Our boss gave each of us the same mission and did not coordinate our efforts. We found that support staff was doing the same work reporting on the work-product progress up two divergent chains of command.

It was something like a matrix structure where one person or team reports to two different managers. However, no single point of contact was in charge; instead, there were two. The relationships were not doubled but multiplied exponentially.

This was a reporting structure that was even more unmanageable. The Big Boss failed to understand this variation of the principle of Unity of Command. The one boss should hold one person accountable for one task.

Count all the men from thirty to fifty years of age who come to serve in the work at the Tent of Meeting. Numbers 4:3

Your Business Professor has reached the status of "a senior gentleman of a certain age," which is diplomatic code for "old guy."

So, I had to do what no young person would need to do. I had to run around more...

on a track.

A couple decades ago, I started to run marathons. But as the miles accumulated on life's odometer, Your Business Professor, like other senior (there's that word again) managers, had to demonstrate that my energy matched my experience, such as it is.

If I was to influence clients I had to rack up the miles, and not just on an airplane. This is still another conundrum for a manager to manage. He has to be old enough to have experience and still young enough To Get Things Done.

As CEO Jack Welch reminds us in the year 2000 GE Annual Report, we must have, "the personal Energy to welcome and deal with the speed of change… and the ability to consistently Execute."

This is the "energy in the one who executes" that Alexander Hamilton outlined in *The Federalist Papers* Number 70. Hamilton, whose image can be seen on the U.S. ten dollar bill, wrote that energy or activity in the presidency is "the leading character in the definition of good government."

French philosopher Montesquieu (1689 to 1755), who is known for the "separation of powers," called this "vigor" in the executive.

Younger people and the manager's younger self really don't need the marathon-mileage demonstration to show energy.

It takes decades to season a CEO. Years of trial and error are needed to refine the practice and the craft of management, which is only improved by, well, practice. Marathons are measured by the mile and are a proxy for energy. So what is the measure of wisdom and judgment?

In the Bible, Numbers 4:3 provides some direction. Count all the men from thirty to fifty years of age who come to serve in the work at the Tent of Meeting.

Jack Weinberg would lead the lunacy of the Free Speech Hippie Movement in 1964 at UC Berkeley. He said, "Don't trust anyone over 30."

The wisdom of the ages would have, of course, a different perspective: "Don't trust anyone under 30" to execute anything important. Joseph was thirty when he was appointed as deputy to the Pharaoh. David was anointed king at thirty. Even Christ went public at that same number of years. (Rowell 1997)

This is simple pattern recognition.

Jesus began his ministry at the age of thirty earning the right to be called "rabbi," or teacher. He managed a group of twelve direct reports and his leadership changed the world.

The United States Constitution is the basis for all of our country's laws. The founding document follows Scripture and sets the minimum age for the CEO of the USA at 35 (a mere pup).

Et tu, Brute? Is it possible to avoid backstabbing office politics?

The CEO was fired. He didn't deliver. Did his staff really help him or "help" him implement needed changes? Was this a problem of leadership or followership? Did he get what he deserved? Or was he sabotaged?

Larry Bossidy and Ram Charan tell the story of Gordon Richard Thoman at Xerox in *Execution: The Discipline of Getting Things Done* (2009). The board of directors of Xerox had rapidly promoted Thoman from COO to the top slot for his leadership and track record containing expenses. He knew how to cut costs. Thoman knew that more positive change was needed and set in place two reorganizational efforts.

The first was to streamline operations from 90-plus administration centers down to four.

The second was a customer refocus by moving from a geographic organization to an industry-specific org chart. The two big changes were long overdue.

Thoman attempted to do both at once. And this might have been possible in another organization. But the "clubby culture" of Xerox's crowd of senior managers "did not take kindly to an outsider." Insiders called it "BuRox" short for 'Bureaucracy-Xerox." (Bossidy 2009)

One gets the sense that this clubby bureaucracy did exactly as the CEO Thoman had directed. He was not well liked and was described as "haughty," as you might expect from a Francophile with a Ph.D. who had been awarded the *Legion of Honour.* Thoman's detached, indifferent demeanor may not have demanded the rigorous debate big changes deserve.

Or perhaps his leadership teams were "yes men" who simply saluted and passed down the orders from on high.

Bureaucratic office politics is an art form in any organization. But at Xerox, infighting under Thoman took on the palette of painter Jackson Pollock—no straight lines and vigorous color splatters. "We will give the boss exactly what he asked for," may have been the Xerox establishment's unsaid response. "And watch the disaster Thoman created."

The "iron cage," as Max Weber called bureaucracies, can lift up any incompetent manager. And can destroy the best and stab any genius in the back.

The manager cannot succeed in execution—if he does not have the support of the bureaucracy.

The manager cannot fail in execution—if he has the support of the bureaucracy.

Yes, the new CEO attempted to do too much too soon. He may not have failed in the planning, but in the leading/motivating. He is ultimately responsible for all the company did or failed to do. He failed in the execution.

★

Consultants Tom Peters and Robert Waterman, Jr. wrote *In Search of Excellence* (1982) and give us background on execution,

> *It is meticulously shifting the attention of the institution through the mundane language of management systems. It is altering agendas so that new priorities get enough attention.*
>
> *It is being visible when things are going awry, and invisible when they are working well.*
>
> *It's listening carefully much of the time, frequently speaking with encouragement, and reinforcing words with believable action. It's being tough when necessary, and it's the occasional naked use of power—*

Daniel Lawrence Whitney has taken implementation, the getting things done from business to show-business in a uniquely American style. He was able to get the execution of *Completed Staff Work* to fit on a bumper sticker. This is Larry the Cable Guy: *Git r Done!*

Execute: is the implementation of the manager's decision. *Completed Staff Work* gets the decision made so that the next phase of the work can begin. This is where good intentions become good work, well done. Execution is getting objectives met, within constraints and often with limited resources.

Discussion Questions
1. Why was Lincoln grateful to have Grant as his general?
2. What are the dangerous assumptions in execution?
3. Plans are not enough for success. Explain.

4. How are "energy" and "execute" related?
5. Does chronological age make a difference? How?
6. Is execution possible without organizational support?
7. Explain the appeal of Larry the Cable Guy, *Git r Done!*

CHAPTER 21

Deadlines: Projects must be on time and on budget.

MY REPORT WAS LATE. AGAIN. It was the weekly summary of the business silo to The Big Boss and Your Business Professor was forever letting the urgent push out the important. I had not learned or developed the habit of meeting that deadline.

Habit: how can we make or break a routine?

So I was late, and the product probably wasn't any good either. Writer Will Durant paraphrased Aristotle, *We are what we repeatedly do. Excellence, then, is not a choice but a habit.* (Durant 1991)

I wasn't getting anything else done or done well. I was beginning to feel like a real manager.

"Managing is a job with a perpetual preoccupation: the manager can never be free to forget the work, never has the pleasure of knowing, even temporarily, that there is nothing left to do." (Mintzberg, 2009)

But in turning in that deliverable I was acting as an individual contributor with an endpoint: My work had to be without error and on time. I needed to form better habits.

Years later, *The New York Times* reporter Charles Duhigg wrote a bestseller, *The Power of Habit: Why We Do What We Do in Life and*

Business. (2012) Duhigg reminds us of cues, routines, and rewards in habit formation.

James Clear, photographer and weightlifter, expands on this theme with memorable alliteration in Reminder, Routine, and Reward: triggers to do the work and how to be happy about it.

The key, says both Clear and Duhigg, is not to create an entirely new lifestyle but to overlay a routine over an existing habit and find a reward.

These days, Your Business Professor will run some fifteen miles each week. And I am doing this without wasting or budgeting additional time. I take the children to their sporting events and I love to watch them practice and compete. I used to sit in the bleachers at the football field. For years, I never noticed that there was a very nice quarter-mile track surrounding the field.

Now I go to the practices and games (stimulus, cue, reminder) and run (habit response) while listening to audiobooks on my smartest of phones. I use GPS software to publicly track my time on the track that is then uploaded onto social media. The app tells me of the quality of my performance and complete strangers congratulate me (reward).

Ralph Waldo Emerson said, "The reward of a thing well done is to have done it." But there are some things we want undone.

As we establish good habits, how can we stop bad habits? As one wag reminded me, Your Business Professor can keep a grudge long beyond its expiration date.

One of my former managers was living rent-free in my head—I could not stop doing the "what-if" scenario until I learned a simple trick. I put a rubber band on my wrist and would snap it every time I thought of him. Thinking of my former Bad Boss was, indeed, a painful reminder. But once my mind and body were in sync and the phantom manager quickly faded, I could then stop beating myself up. I put a snap to it.

Sometimes the triggers can be painful and useful reminders. Dieters will sometimes skip meals to control gluttony and this could produce a tangible reward. But it could also be a habit stimulus. "Fasting can serve as an automatic reminder to pray," says singer and writer Steve Chapman (2012).

My deliverance of the report to The Big Boss became more consistent when I merged two tasks. Even though the report was due at the close of business on Fridays, I decided to hand it in earlier in the day as I met with a standing appointment with other staffers.

The reminder was the physical meeting "deadline," the response was to bring the report and deliver it to another office, and my reward to myself was a victory lap at the cafeteria and a Snickers® candy bar.

Every racecourse has a finish line. Every event needs a time limit.

For example, Your Business Professor has been a member of a number of Bible study groups and most of them did not end well.

They would form and enthusiastically meet once a week or so. But then they go on; drag on, for a year or more and members would drift away. There was no closure. There were no goalposts.

We could have learned something from Mötley Crüe. What does that rock group and well-run Bible studies have in common?

They know when and how to quit.

A writer for *Fast Company*, Josh Rottenberg, interviewed Mötley Crüe band members. Rottenberg quotes co-founder, bassist, and songwriter Nikki Sixx on an unusual (show) business practice. (05.28.14) The cutting-edge periodical writes that the rock group, "held a press conference to announce their retirement,"

> To add to the air of finality, each member publicly signed a "cessation of touring agreement" that prevents any of them from performing under the Crüe name…The final tour…will give fans a chance to say goodbye and the band a chance to bow out on its own terms.
>
> "We're smart enough to realize that at some point the wheels are going to start to come off the bus—and that's just not a good look," says Sixx.

Mötley Crüe was, well, a class act. They went out with a bang. The endpoint came and they didn't fade away in their black t-shirts. They celebrated.

Small groups like Bible studies, work teams, and special projects should be set up and chartered for a fixed period or a fixed assignment. When the time is up, as in a football's time clock, or when the laps/iterations are completed as in baseball's innings, the books are closed and success is celebrated.

At the endpoint, there should be cheers with a victory lap; every company needs celebration, a commemoration to make a memory at the finish and the beginning. Author and consultant Lorin Woolfe writes about the ancient leader of Israel, King Hezekiah, and his use of ritual:

> As the offering began, singing to the Lord began also, accompanied by trumpets…burnt offering completed. 2 Chronicles 29:28

Anyone who has ever been to a sales meeting or corporate "pep rally" can see some parallels here.

The clothes are different (Brooks Brothers and Armani rather than linen robes), as are the musical instruments, and hopefully there are fewer live sacrifices. But the major commonality remains: dedication to and celebration of purpose. (Woolfe 2002)

Good managers don't move the goalposts when the game is over. They tear them down in a boisterous riot and get ready for the next game.

Seven days from now I will send rain on the earth for forty days and forty nights, and I will wipe from the face of the earth every living creature I have made. Genesis 7:4

The world was coming to an end at midnight December 31, 1999. We had planned for it for years. It was, as one techno-wag said, "a disaster with a deadline."

The Year 2000 rollover was going to be big worldwide. No escape. Like the flood, we knew it was coming.

We knew this would be no mere technology challenge to be solved with exceptional American ingenuity. The Year 2000 was problematic with unknown unknowns. No internet connection. Cell phones dead. The power grid dark.

Armageddon.

In the late 1990s one-half of the world's internet traffic passed through the Commonwealth of Virginia, thanks to America Online—AOL.com. And maybe another northern Virginia entity in Arlington: the Pentagon. I think that was a secret.

Your Business Professor had the Y2K responsibility for Health and Human Resources, a $5 billion enterprise in the Virginia government. The boss, Governor Jim Gilmore, a former military intelligence officer, knew what was possible and not possible to combat the Y2K Bug.

There was a lot we couldn't do. And it wasn't all technology.

It was a condition of continued employment that there was to be no interruption or adverse incidents to the citizens of the Commonwealth and the rest of the World.

(We worker-bees could not get it wrong. The world ends *and* we'd get a bad employee appraisal. A subpar job performance would not be a simple career-ending/world-ending mistake. Going out with a bang, so to say.)

Business literature notes the adrenaline rush of the "peak experience." The Office of Governor of Virginia had this as he had The Whole World in His Hands.

The web had to run for the wide world and more: Virginia's hospital doors had to remain open and the prison doors closed. Fresh water and waste water valves had to direct flow in the correct and desired directions.

Local first responders had to be able to coordinate communications across jurisdictional silos. Governor Gilmore was among the first to realize the importance of seamless radio traffic between Fed-State-Local law enforcement. (It still wouldn't be fixed years later, as documented on 9/11.)

There were lots of challenges beyond government resources. So Gilmore hired the biggest IT consulting firms on the planet and bought their solutions packages. In my weekly staff meetings, I had a dozen of the smartest experts in the business. I was not one of them.

They let me think I was in control at the head of the table. Maybe I was, but these consultants wouldn't let me, a mere bureaucrat, make a mistake.

Virginia spent $215 million and nothing happened here or elsewhere. There were some problems in Nigeria. We now think it was some kind of scam.

Nothing crashed, except for that super-secret three-letter-agency satellite…and some defibrillators. It was not my fault, and no one died.

The lesson learned was that managing technology was the easy part. The cost is high and penalties severe when deadlines are missed. The real challenge is in managing projects—through people—on time and on budget.

It always is.

To get better execution, the manager might do *less* thinking.

Social scientists studied the behavior of children on two different playgrounds surrounded by streets in an inner city. One playground had a perimeter fence. The other had no fence, no protective boundary.

In the fenced-in area the children ran, explored, and went wild from edge to fenced-edge. It was utter creative chaos, but very safe.

On the other hand, in the boundaryless playground, in the open field, the children bunched in the center not daring to venture near the sides with vehicular traffic close by. The children were unfettered and terrified. Their movement was uncontrolled and not safe.

Science demonstrated that the children felt freer within a fence. Fences made for more fun. The children did not have to worry or think about the danger of running out of the park into oncoming traffic. **Oddly, the fence is made for freedom and freedom of thought.**

Tim Brown, the CEO and president of IDEO, says his firm specializes in creativity. The industrial design firm will often generate new concepts within existing systems and strict guidelines. We often think that the best creative minds will sit for weeks stroking their chins as they Think Out of the Box. IDEO does no such thing.

The creative company's managers will sometimes give their teams only a few hours to generate New Ideas. Tight and restrictive timelines produce a better product.

Life and work are easier if decisions can be made routine within guidelines. Any task, even the "right thing to do," is easy to implement after the decision is made.

Standard operating procedures, or SOPs in business and the military, reduce the amount of thinking a person has to do. Decision-making is reduced to rote habits that don't consume active or new thought processes. Like an efficient technology, we do not want employees to run out of buffer space. Procedural guardrails can keep routine projects from falling off the edge of a cliff.

Scripture has ten simple SOPs. When they're followed, they can ease emotional anguish of attempting to avoid the wrong actions. We know them as the Ten Commandments.

After we avoid the bad, how do we plan for the good? To do the right things, right?

Entrepreneur Richard Koch says, "...to ensure that the project team does only the really high-value tasks, *impose an impossible time scale,*

> *Faced with an impossible time scale, [project members] will identify and implement the 20 percent of the requirements that delivers 80 percent of the benefit.*
>
> *Again, it is the inclusion of the "nice to have" features that turn potentially sound projects into looming catastrophes.*
>
> *Impose stretch targets. Desperate situations inspire creative solutions. Ask for a prototype in four weeks. Demand a live pilot in three months.*

This will force the development team to apply the 80/20 rule and really make it work. Take calculated risks. (Koch 1998, 2008)

This is an update on Pareto's Principle and the rule applies to most all areas. For example, managers understand that 20 percent of their team will produce 80 percent of the results. And 80 of the manager's problems will be caused by 20 percent of their staffers.

To get the best execution consider a narrow framework and short time frames. Do you want your staff to explore a playground of solutions? Put up a fence.

An effective charity will leave it all on the field.

The charity had given away its last dollar, shut down its website, released its employees, and turned off its phones.

The John M. Olin Foundation had been very good to my kith and kin. The charity had awarded generous grants to wife Charmaine, as she completed her doctorate in political science at the University of Virginia.

So we were surprised when this conservative charity emptied its endowment and closed up shop. But this was the plan all along. The benefactor, John Olin, directed that the work of his foundation would continue indefinitely only through the legacy of the recipients. Olin did not want his foundation to exist in perpetuity—forever dispensing grants.

He feared that future generations might not honor his wish of supporting free market thinkers.

Grant making foundations, over time, will sometimes appoint trustees who lean away from the original mission of the organization, violating donor intent. Olin wanted to avoid this. He directed that the foundation's assets be dispersed within a single generation of his death, which occurred in 1982. The last grant was made in 2005.

This is the lesson for leaders. Even the largest projects must have an endpoint, a completion date. All races have a well defined line with a checkered flag waved with a flourish. The major milestones of achieving a goal and completing a vision must be celebrated and followed by focusing on new horizons.

John Olin's vision lives on in the work of the universities, think tanks, and scholars he supported. My family is forever grateful.

From the other side of eternity Olin can quote 2 Timothy 4:7, *I have fought the good fight, I have finished the race, I have kept the faith.*

Do not eat the food of a begrudging host, do not crave his delicacies; for he is the kind of person who is always thinking about the cost. "Eat and drink," he says to you, but his heart is not with you. Proverbs 23: 6-7

Middle managers need to be appreciated, just like normal people.

Bob got the job. It was a promotion from within the company to management. "Welcome to the overhead," said the human resources junior vice president. He wasn't smiling.

The HR VP was concerned about the additional payroll and that headcount would not be reduced. He didn't see Bob's worth to the organization. The personnel manager would fit playwright Oscar Wilde's definition of a cynic: "A man who knows the price of everything and the value of nothing."

Our newly minted manager loved his work and never needed to know about the amateur managers in his chain of command. Bob should have considered the actions of the CEO and the team he put in place. Yes, the boss was smart enough to see Bob's potential, but was blind to the dangers of the cheapskate VP. He would soon see that he was in the company of scrooges.

Controlling, as the textbooks tell us, is, "the management function for monitoring performance and making needed changes." (Bateman 2012) And changes were a-coming. After a month on the job our new manager, Bob, was called into a meeting with his twelve peer managers. They were each directed to cut their expenses by 8 percent.

The number was "fair." Each manager got the same number. But it wasn't right. Bob's product was about to take off and he needed more resources, not fewer.

An across-the-board reduction is not sound leadership. That is too easy. Share the pain; everyone suffers regardless of opportunity or nonperformance. It is the socialism of the Little League participation trophy.

In contrast, a good boss makes tough decisions for the right business unit at the right time. This is hard labor. Peter Drucker warns,

> *There are no formulas for making the decisions on managed expenditures. They must always be based on judgment and are almost always a compromise.*
>
> *But even a wrong decision is better than a haphazard approach "by bellows and meat ax": inflating appropriations in fair weather and cutting them off as soon as the first cloud appears. (Drucker 1954)*

Peter Drucker would observe that, "Enterprises that succeed in being change leaders make sure that they staff the opportunities." (Drucker 2009)

Deadlines: are met by managers who get projects completed on time and on budget. This is the finish line, an end date, a goal line where performance is recorded on a scoreboard. A deadline is a limitation that, counterintuitively, will unleash greater creativity than an open-ended timeline.

Discussion Questions
1. Virtue is a habit. Explain.
2. Establishing a habit can have three parts. Define them.
3. Every racecourse has a finish line. Why is this important?
4. Why do fences make playgrounds more fun?
5. Why are SOPs important?
6. How does the 80/20 rule help creativity?
7. Deadlines are a control measure. Explain this management component.

PART FOUR:

Presentation—How Do I
Persuade My Manager?

CHAPTER 22

Sales: The transference of emotion.

AT ITS CORE, *COMPLETED STAFF Work* is a sales process. The Memo is a sales document. Leaders and Followers need to sell up and down the organizational chain-of-command and across bureaucratic business silos. Leadership and Followership in business can learn from the sales process. *Completed Staff Work* needs a MAP: Money, Authority, and Pain.

Money. A staffed-out recommendation includes the consideration: the favors exchanged or budget allotted. Money, or something like it, changes hands. The staffer should know, *how much political capital is needed?*

Authority. The decision-maker usually has the authority to spend money. But this will need to be checked.

Pain. People will avoid pain before moving to pleasure. Find the pain. Then learn if it hurts—bad. A decision is easier to secure when a problem has a solution to stop the pain. (Sandler 1996)

Attention: a sale can only be made when the seller has caught the eye of the prospective buyer.

Your Business Professor had been regularly calling on a particular hospital account making dozens of sales presentations. I had known the decision-maker, a nurse, for years. She asked me, "Do you have a 26-gauge?"

I stared at her. My small business was the only company on the market that manufactured the neonatal needles for premature babies. And I had told her that dozens of times in dozens of sales pitches.

She had been paying little attention to me, and I wasn't able to tell the story. I was little more than a professional visitor. All of my company's marketing efforts, budget, and my personal selling genius were dust in the whirlwind that was her Intensive Care Unit. My glossy, four-color direct mail piece did not catch any attention either. She did not hear me.

I was selling the Good News of teeny-tiny catheters for intravenous therapy, but no one had ears to hear. No one was buying my copy.

Recent literature and studies confirm ancient understanding. In an 1898 issue of *Printers' Ink*, a writer noted, "The mission of an advertisement is to sell goods. To do this, it must attract attention …" (Wikipedia 2015)

Later, in the June 2, 1921, publication of *Printers' Ink* sales trainer C. P. Russell wrote, "How to Write a Sales-Making Letter." He said that selling could be best done after the salesman has first gained Attention from the customer, then Interest, Desire, and Action.

This popular formula has made its way into countless modern marketing textbooks under the rubric-acronym AIDA. (Wikipedia 2015 citing Russell 1921)

Management of the sales process is successful when a deal is done, the sale is closed, and the account opened. Sales representatives as account managers are the best communicators; they accomplish organization goals with the active support of their company's customers. They get attention both inside and outside their organizations.

The best sales professionals using *Completed Staff Work* get noticed. People listen.

Your Business Professor was an account manager in a start-up selling a tangible product—machinery. I was acting as a rainmaker where I performed all the actions of both marketing and sales. I studied under an experienced sales trainer, George, whose last name is lost to the decades.

He encouraged a simple method to catch the attention of the prospect and provoke some action with—literally—a sales "pitch." He threw an attachment, usually a lightweight bolt, at the customer. Now, it was a gentle, high arch toss, released after George had his potential buyer's eye. After they caught his pitch, George always caught the buyer's attention. And when the prospect had made the catch, it was easier for him to see and feel the product features to— most importantly—hear and understand the customer benefits.

Let us return to my nurse-with-purchasing-authority. A beeping monitor distracted her. But I answered her question, "Yes, we have the 26-gauge." My hands were full. I clumsily pulled a product sample from my bag and asked her, "Can you open this for me?"

She didn't drop the ball.

I had her active attention; she finally heard the message and the deal was done.

The recruiter said, "$150k base—with a track record of success in hospitals with consultative sales skills."

Consulting? I thought. *Giving advice is selling?*

Who knew?

I didn't get the job.

But I was able to land a position with a more modest base salary. I was new and had only a vague notion of the saying in business that, "Nothing happens until somebody sells something." I would learn soon enough. It was my first big sales job. I would be cold-calling on physicians. But my manager wasn't demanding sales numbers, just behaviors. I was being trained as a consultant to advise clients.

The sales training was not what I expected. The sales trainer was not Alec Baldwin in the movie *Glengarry Glen Ross*, pounding the ABCs of AIDA (sales-speak for "Always Be Closing" and "Attention, Interest, Desire, Action").

Sales, my new trainer explained, was more than FAB. Selling was not just:

- Features: describing what product is.
- Advantages: what it does.
- Benefits: the value to the customer.

Instead, my trainer and mentor taught two basics:

- Think behaviors, not "dollars" and
- Practice influence, don't "sell."

High-end selling taught me that selling/persuading is first about behaviors. Get your behaviors right, and a customer and the money should follow.

The sales funnel statistics were simple. At the top, at the widest part of the funnel, were the actions that I had to perform as a condition of employment. The part was easy; visit three hospitals a day, meet three new clinicians per hospital, for five days a week.

It didn't matter what happened. No one interested? I just had to bang on doors (just as in my old days in selling door-to-door).

This behavior, I was assured, would lead to relationships, finding pain, solving problems, and creating customers.

The company numbers worked for me. As I got better, the sales dollars got bigger.

The second skill my mentor taught was to influence, to persuade. Good sales training programs remind us the first step in the sales process is to establish rapport. The prospect must respond to you, and then trust you.

Earning the confidence of the prospect begins with the other person making a move in the salesman's direction. In most sales, that microscopic move was getting the prospect to respond to an email, then an in-person conversation and to sit still and ask questions.

If you're not knocking on doors, what might that small move look like? That first response could be getting an electronic reply. If the prospect will not open the door, answer the phone, or return an email, there is no relationship. And there will be no sale.

Please understand, I am not minimizing the skills and the teachable science of salesmanship. Rather, I learned in cold calling that sales include the art and craft of personal interactions. And this principle, of course, has broad application for management challenges.

Inconsistency or the wrong combination of what is offered and then delivered can leave a bad taste.

The saltwater taffy candy tasted terrible. It was safe to eat and would hurt nothing but sales. And it was my fault.

Your (much younger) Business Professor did it on purpose. It started as a noble experiment but then devolved into a base prank.

One summer, I was working as a candy cook with two other bored confederates. We dreamed up a chemistry research project combining two of the five senses: color coordination and a taste response. No animals were hurt in this human testing.

Our hypothesis was simple, "If the taste and coloring were different, would the tongue *taste* what the eye saw? Or would the eye *see* what the tongue tasted?"

So we mixed the purple coloring with the lemon flavoring, instead of with the grape.

And we combined the yellow lemon coloring with the grape flavoring. This produced a mixed-message that tasted awful, or so I was told.

We dreamed of getting published in the *Journal of Food Science*. But we lost interest and I would later go on to the next best thing: sales and marketing. (Who would think anything "saltwater" would taste good? Now that's marketing management genius.)

But we did prove the old sales training maxim, often attributed to Zig Ziglar, that says, "A confused mind always says no."

The taster had to think about it … and too much thinking—overthinking—is dangerous. [2]

Positive is easy. Contraindications are not. Mixed taste is a negative. The confusion, the inconsistency takes a fraction of a second longer for the human mind to process. A positive experience can be processed fast. A negative experience takes longer.

To be clearer, authors Gary Mack and David Casstevens wrote in their go-to sports psychology book *Mind Gym* (2002) that, "Doubts cause intellectual confusion. Doubts can be paralyzing."

The best managers avoid the confusion of mixed messages and have one theme. One voice reduces risk for the good of the company and community. And author-entrepreneur-marketer Seth

---

2   *The overthinking part was not dangerous to me. The mixed-up saltwater taffy tasted just fine. I am partially colorblind.*

Godin reminds us that, "Consumers are too good at sniffing out inconsistencies..."

Unless you're trying to cause trouble.

In the mid-1970s, IBM was noted for inducing fear, uncertainty, and doubt, or FUD, into the decision process of buyers considering purchasing a competitive product. If a buyer had concerns about a computer company—even if those concerns were introduced by a competing vendor—the purchaser would slow down and then not consider a new supplier.

The adage (possibly promoted by IBM) said, "No one was ever fired for buying IBM." Purchasing agents were fearful of buying anything else. FUD at its finest.

Management textbook writer Thomas S. Bateman notes that planning activities include the ability to, "Analyze current situation. Anticipate the future. Determine objectives. Decide on what actions to engage in. Choose a business strategy. Determine resources to achieve goals." (2012) This is *Completed Staff Work*.

Planning is easy if you have a single objective, unless the cooks in the kitchen making fud(ge) take you in two different directions.

The best action or tactic to sell a recommendation in *Completed Staff Work* is to make a personal report. This is a face-to-face sales presentation—where you must be there in person.

Yahoo! CEO Marissa Mayer and her HR department explain,

> *We need to be working side-by-side...Some of the best decisions and insights come from hallway and cafeteria discussions, meeting new people and impromptu team meetings.*
>
> *Speed and quality are often sacrificed when we work from home. We need to be one Yahoo, and that starts with physically being together. (Carlson 2016)*

Births, deaths, and marriages each demand personal attendance. They cannot be 'phoned-in.' So too with important business events and meetings. This is the limitation to the trend toward remote work and telework. The personal touch can only be done in person.

And finally, persistence. Your Business Professor has been on both sides of the table as buyer and seller in the business of procurement. I am often asked, *When does the salesperson make a pest of himself?*

The answer is, *not soon enough*.

And after getting to a real, *no*.

The art of selling is knowing when to quit and move on to the next opportunity. Not investing too much valuable time in someone who does not have any "Pain."

But sales reps often quit too soon. They bail out of a meeting before they get tossed out.

Qualifying the customer "to go for the no" where there is direct questioning is a learned skill and not for the faint of heart. I would advise some on my sales team that, *If you're not getting thrown out of an account once a month, you're not working hard enough.* For most of my sales reps, I was just joking. But I was serious for some.

Sales is the transference of emotion. A good idea, well researched and well presented, is only sold when there is "buy-in" from the boss. In every interaction someone is purchasing and someone is selling. After the manager has bought into a project, he will need it to the wider team, across business silos and the stakeholders. This will be easy since the Alert Staffer "wired" the proposal with all concerned beforehand.

Discussion Questions

1. What is sales?
2. How does selling work in *Completed Staff Work*?
3. What does MAP stand for? Explain.
4. What do ABC and FAB stand for? Define.
5. Why would IBM push FUD?
6. What is "Consultative Selling"?
7. Why does selling in person have the highest close rate?
8. Always go to an office. Never work at home. Why?
9. Where is the line between persistence and knowing when to quit?

CHAPTER 23

Communication: Data exchange is a two-way street.

WHAT IS THE FIRST FUNCTION of the executive?

My mission in combat arms was simple, "Move, Shoot, and Communicate." Who knew war-fighting was so much like corporate America?

The military is perhaps the world's best training platform to learn and study the practice of management. Your Business Professor learned the value of the "net" while in the Army years before the internet became commonplace and our current worldwide web of connectivity. Every small Army unit was connected by a secure radio network to maintain contact with superiors and subordinates.

It didn't matter how competent a team was in mobility or marksmanship if the group was not connected and in communication with sister units and the boss. The unit could not be considered to be combat effective unless it was online.

Once radio contact was made by gaining permission to join the net, with authentication, the work of the senior commander could continue. He had many parts to play and communication was at the center of the web,

"There are three roles that all managers perform," Thomas Bateman from the University of Virginia writes,

> *Interpersonal, as leader, liaison, figurehead;*
> *Informational, as monitor, disseminator, spokesman; and*
> *Decisional, as entrepreneur, disturbance handler, negotiator.*
> *(Bateman 2013)*

Each of these demands the ability to send and receive data both in person and electronically.

And this is nonstop, even if it's redundant. The great writer Dr. Samuel Johnson said, "People need to be reminded more than they need to be instructed."

Professor Henry Mintzberg of McGill University says (2009),

> *Watch any manager and one thing readily becomes apparent: the amount of time that is spent simply communicating—namely, collecting and disseminating information for its own sake, without necessarily processing it.*

Talk and technology were about to explode in the 1920s. Herbert Hoover was the first president to have a telephone on his desk. Earlier presidents would have one secretary. He had five. There was a lot more communicating to do. (Manchester 1973) And even that was not enough. Hoover was still blamed for the Great Depression beginning in 1929.

Chester Barnard, president of New Jersey Bell Telephone in the early 1900s, identified the "first executive function" as "to develop and maintain a system of communication." (Mintzberg 2009)

The manager spends his day in communication, so that means he's got to be a real talker? Right?

Maybe so. According to Professor Mintzberg, managing is "between 60 and 90 percent oral." Jeanne Liedtka at the Darden School, University of Virginia says, "Talk is the technology of leadership." (Mintzberg 2009)

The manager will have to do better than Wendell L. Willkie. He did not pace himself and lost his voice during the presidential campaign in 1940. This made his run even more difficult against the practiced FDR. (Manchester 1973)

President Ronald Reagan, known as the Great Communicator, spent decades practicing the craft of delivering the lines of a speech. He knew how to present the aura of optimism, that, under his leadership, we would have a new morning in America.

And we did. Because he said so.

...Day and night they never stop saying: "'Holy, holy, holy is the Lord God Almighty,' who was, and is, and is to come." Book of Revelation 4:8b

Repetition: just because the manager said it once does not mean the staffer heard it.

The reporters were bored. They had heard the same speech a dozen times. But segments of speech were still picked up and presented as news. Potential voters had "heard" the speech before, but then some finally heard the speech.

Day and night they never stop saying...

My wife Charmaine was a senior advisor to Mike Huckabee during his presidential run in 2008. Your Business Professor followed them around, driving the mobile-homeschool-truck with our five children.

We would watch the crowd's reaction to Huckabee's speeches.

Most of the attendees in the crowd were enthusiastic supporters, but occasionally a voter's eyes would light up; a face would lift up and the message would be received, understood, and, finally, heard.

Repetition and reiteration catch a listener's attention. This can be done in spoken communication but not so much on paper. Repeating a written phrase on a hard copy script will not work. What sounds melodious over the air to the ear looks odd on paper to the eye. Repetition is an audible exercise.

George Bernard Shaw said, "Tell 'em what you're gonna tell 'em. Tell 'em. Then tell 'em what you told 'em."

But I repeat myself...

Jack Welch and his wife, former *Harvard Business Review* editor-in-chief Suzy Welch, remind us in LinkedIn (2014) to "Over-Communicate,"

> *It's your job to communicate your message...over and over and over again...Even when you're ready to gag over the message, you have to keep communicating it.*
>
> *Just because you say something once, it doesn't mean it's going to happen. Too often, managers think, "Hey, I told my team what to do." ... But you also have to make it your mission to follow up — relentlessly — to see that things are moving in the right direction.*

Holy, Holy, Holy, is the Lord God Almighty...

Alliteration helps the reiteration as when Julius Caesar stayed within the 140 Twitter character limit reporting one of his military victories, "*Veni, vidi, vici.*" I came, I saw, I conquered.

' who was, and is,

Consultant Tom Peters wrote in *Fast Company*,

> *Leadership takes an almost bottomless supply of verbal energy: working the phones, staying focused on your message, repeating the same mantra until you can't stand the sound of your own voice—and then repeating it some more, because just when you start to become*

bored witless with the message, it's probably starting to seep into the organization. (Woolfe 2002)

and is to come."

The professional manager will repeat a message until it is heard in the ear, then to the brain where it can be sounded in the heart.

When words are many, sin is not absent, but he who holds his tongue is wise, Proverbs 10:19

Stop and wait: more is said in the silence.

Mitt Romney walked to the podium. A noisy crowd was shouting encouragement as he was considering a run for president. The sweating mass would not hush but Romney would not be rushed. He smiled and let the loud rollicking continue. But he did have a speech to give.

He stood at the microphone and smiled at the throng. He waited. Silent. It was a pregnant pause because something good was going to happen.

The practiced Massachusetts governor did not speak until the room exhausted itself and went silent, waiting on his words.

As eloquent as he was with the use of words, he was even better with the use of silence. William Shakespeare said, "*I stand in pause where I shall first begin.*" Napoleon would wait and hold for 40 seconds before beginning a speech. This is command presence.

Author James C. Humes in *Speak Like Churchill, Stand Like Lincoln: 21 Powerful Secrets of History's Greatest Speakers,* calls this quietness the "Power Pause" and "Strategic Silence." It takes self-confidence and, like all public speaking, it takes practice.

Your Business Professor was once coached by an executive search firm for an interview. The counselor advised me to appropriately pause. I don't remember if I got the job.

But I. Would. Remember. Making. Every. Dramatic. Pause.

It felt funny the first time. The silence only lasted four seconds. In practicing a speech the speaker should count out: one thousand and one, one thousand and two… It will feel like an eternity. Four seconds is usually enough to quiet your group and get their attention. If for no other reason than people will look at you to learn if you are having a heart attack.

Because that's what it feels like.

I have experimented on the four-second-silent-rule with my classes and it works. Four seconds of quiet from a professor is exactly how long it takes a student to stop texting and look up from his iPhone.

James Humes, one of Ronald Reagan's speechwriters, tells aspiring Great Communicators (2009),

> *Before you speak, try to lock your eyes on each of your soon-to-be listeners…Every second you wait will strengthen the impact of your opening words…Stand, stare, and command your audience, and they will bend their ears to listen.*

The Army Chief of Staff during WWII, General George Marshall, used this silent treatment. When starting a meeting,

> *Marshall said nothing. He simply gazed across the room…not saying a word or making a gesture. (Mosley 1982)*

Use silence before beginning a talk, silence before answering a question, and silence before beginning a new thought.

And finally, don't step on your laugh lines. Stop and wait for the reaction. Jack Benny, the famed vaudeville-radio-television funnyman, had impeccable comedic timing. At the punch line of a joke he would stop.

And wait.

And bring his hand to his face and scan the audience until they got the joke, and the crowd laughed together.

Romney ran for president and did not win. The other candidate with even better oratory skills won.

Groom your own "Napoleon's Corporal: communicate the vision with a simple written plan.

Napoleon Bonaparte was a genius in leadership with a simple tactic for getting his vision communicated. He won by having his battle plans understood by his staff. Simple. Indeed, every business unit leader wishes it were easy.

Napoleon had hundreds of thousands of men in the French *grande armée*. And not a single cell phone. How did he get his message communicated and understood?

Simple.

Bonaparte and his staff invested considerable effort formulating a course of action before each battle. This always involved complicated timing and logistics. But complexity is a loser in war and in business.

Napoleon knew that his troops—down to the lowest levels—had to grasp the plan. It had to be understood. It had to be simple. How did the Emperor of the French, commanding a vast army, do a comprehension test of his preparations?

Legend has it that Napoleon kept a low-ranking enlisted man on his general staff. The staffer was not the sharpest soldier in the field; he was actually quite dull. And that's why he was retained. Before Bonaparte issued any order, he had this dullard—the slowest thinking man in the army—read the directive. If Napoleon's corporal could understand it, only then did the genius general release the written orders to his field commanders.

It is not known if the French general and conqueror of Europe could recite Habakkuk 2:2, although he practiced its preaching, *"Write down the revelation and make it plain on tablets so that a herald may run with it."*

Napoleon did believe that, *The Bible is no mere book, but a living creature, with a power that conquers all that oppose it.*

Keep it Simple.

Communication is the transmission and the reception of information. This is a skill requiring practice and refinement. This two-way interaction of useful data is seen and heard, of course, but is so much more. Communication includes any signaling of written, spoken, and nonverbal imaging or presentation.

Discussion Questions
1. What is the first function of the executive? Why?
2. What are the three roles of the manager?
3. Who was the first president to have a phone on his desk? Explain.
4. Why is repetition necessary?
5. What is the value of Napoleon's corporal?
6. Silence commands attention. How?
7. Communication is two-way. Explain
8. What is the "Power Pause?"

CHAPTER 24

Inertia: Get your manager moving in your direction.

Present your case, says the LORD. Set forth your arguments, says Jacob's King.

Isaiah 41:21

MOVING EMOTION; MANAGEMENT MUST DEMAND persuasion.

"I agree with you, I want to do it, now make me do it," said FDR.

After winning his first presidential election in 1932 Franklin Delano Roosevelt met with the like-minded Socialists who worked to get him elected. The supporters had an agenda, something to sell to the incoming administration. And FDR was excited about the numerous proposals and was eager to get started implementing his New Deal. Roosevelt worked to get off to a fast start in confronting the Great Depression using relief, recovery, and reform.

During FDR's first 100 days, Congress approved his every request.

How did he accomplish this?

Roosevelt was expert in the exercise of influence. It was not just his projection of power but in his insistence on being persuaded, "Now make me do it." He asked to be "sold" on a course of action. He expected the best possible debate and argument and recommendations. He was demanding *Completed Staff Work.*

This sounds much like Isaiah 41:21, *Present your case,* says the LORD. *Set forth your arguments,* says Jacob's King.

It is the responsibility of the President to get the best possible advice in the crafting and implementing of policy. However, the president does not have to "buy" anything presented to him. FDR insisted that the initiatives had to be 'sold' to him in such a compelling fashion that he would have little choice but to adopt the proposal.

The president was looking for good policies and the frameworks that would link together competing interests in government and the private sector. He wanted win-win-win solutions using limited resources with an obvious path to success.

Not all agree on the results of FDR's decisions, but all acknowledge his ability to get things done through the thinking support of others.

A complete sales pitch makes management decisions easy.

A proper introduction can get the manager to make a move.

Politicians offer a lesson on getting an audience with a decision-maker. Thomas Phillip "Tip" O'Neill, Jr., the late Speaker of the House during Reagan's presidency, was the complete Irishman from eastern Massachusetts. He was captain of his high school basketball team. He loved politics and people. But the boss from Boston didn't love just anybody.

The position of any politico skilled in elective office or in office politics is the ability to dispense favors or perquisites. This is an exercise in influence and indirect control.

Favors have value in their scarcity and are best awarded when the action of one reward can satisfy multiple constituents. The Speaker was always able to satisfy at least two people with every favor dispensed.

How did this consummate leader do it?

The senior congressman had a simple directive for his gatekeeping staff to welcome supplicants,

"Don't take nobody nobody brought."

Interviews with the Speaker were granted only if a trusted third party made the introduction—usually a friend known well by both the Speaker and the seeker of the favor. If the courtesy was granted it had a double effect. O'Neill would endear himself to old friend and new friend alike with a single act of generosity.

This tactic was both brilliant and effective.

Politics, business, and the Gospel are done best with the Tip O'Neill multiplier effect. The professional can make things happen with an introduction as cited in Matthew 10:40, *Anyone who welcomes you welcomes me, and anyone who welcomes me welcomes the one who sent me.*

Big wins start with small victories.

"We accumulate victories," says Troy Newman who runs a nonprofit. He gets considerable results through little gains and channeling big emotion. Big wins are always desirable; the grand slam home run is spectacular.

But the big homer doesn't come often. The safer sign might be for bunt. The small win. Get on base.

American author Ella Wheeler Wilcox (1850 to 1919) reminds us, "Laugh, and the world laughs with you; weep, and you weep alone." Defeated? And you want to publicly cry about it? That's why God gave us showers to go to sob in. No, we want to win, shouts of victory, drenched from the Gatorade bucket.

Biographer Eric Metaxas writes on winning and the fickleness of the crowd,

> *Bonhoeffer wrote about the way people worship success...It was success they wanted, success more than anything. In Ethics, he wrote, "The world will allow itself to be subdued only by success. It is not ideas or opinions which decide, but deeds." (Metaxas 2010)*

Arthur C. Brooks, president of the American Enterprise Institute (AEI), writes on this measurement of success,

> *Joseph Schumpeter, often called the godfather of modern entrepreneurship, said of entrepreneurs, "The financial result is a secondary consideration." It is, however, "an index of success and a... symptom of victory." (Brooks 2012)*

So how do managers and staffers get business success in the currency of the company, and advance organizational goals? They need a consuming passion for small wins in the right direction—using desire, training, practice, habit, and execution.

The first measure is the desire, the fire-in-the-belly. Do the unit and the management want the goal? Does the staff want to learn how? A learning organization is, "skilled at creating, acquiring, and transferring knowledge, and at modifying its behavior to reflect new knowledge and insights." (Bateman 2013)

Second, is training. The staff and leadership must want to learn more and to improve skills by demanding "continuous learning." This is the growth Carol S. Dweck, Ph.D. explains in her book *Mindset.*

Third, practice.

Fourth, habit. The experienced manager can ignite the desire and set the priorities and direction for the unit's efforts. And movement begins and need not be flawless as long as the first steps are taken and the habit is developed. John Bunyan (1628 to 1688) wrote *Pilgrim's Progress;* not *Pilgrim's Perfection.* The manager's journey resembles Christian's passage. It may not pretty, but it is a start.

The accumulation of victories is best done in short order. Small successes completed fast. The ideal for most staff is a tiny block done a little bit every day. What will I do every day to meet this challenge?

One-A-Day® Vitamins reminds us with clever labeling that the value in their product is the habitual one-tablet-taken-every-single-day. Taking seven tablets on Sunday is not helpful.

A daily routine is formed when the consumer becomes uncomfortable if the vitamin is not taken. Habits are, well, habit-forming.

Big wins are best achieved with a small, daily win. We might not be able to move the manager to get started on a Big Project. But he or she can be encouraged with a low-risk, small-budget pilot project.

This action-tactic works in any direction. This incremental movement works for the staffer to influence his manager. But "small moves" is also an effective way for the manager to lead his team. This is how "employee buy-in" is developed.

Blue Ocean Strategy Institute co-directors W. Chan Kim and Renée Mauborgne, write,

> *Engagement means involving individuals in the decisions that affect them by asking for their input and allowing them to refute the merits of one another's ideas and assumptions. Engagement communicates management's respect for individuals and their ideas.*

Proverbs 25:15a will be at work anywhere on the org chart, *Through patience a ruler can be persuaded...*

Inertia: is getting your manager to move in your direction. Starting—the beginning is the most challenging feature of a project—to "get off the dime" to "take the first step" to "get the ball rolling." The Alert Staffer understands how to get the boss in gear and get moving. This is done easily and safely with the "baby-step" of a pilot project that has a reduced risk and can show a quick win.

Discussion Questions
1. How did FDR succeed?
2. "Tip" O'Neill did not meet with just anyone. How did he decide whom to meet?
3. Bonhoeffer wrote that deeds are more respected than ideas. Explain.
4. What does One-A-Day® Vitamin mean to you?
5. Why is employee engagement important?

CHAPTER 25

U-nO-Dir: Unless Otherwise Directed.

THE DOCTRINE OF *U-NO-DIR* (YOU-KNOW-DEAR) is an essential component of unlocking the power of *Completed Staff Work*. The staffer can ask for and earn this permission to exercise initiative. And the manager should groom his staffers to take on more complicated tasks and decisions. This is where the staffer takes action as a default, unless stopped by his manager.

But first the boss needs to understand the problem. He needs to know that he cannot do it all.

To delegate is to assign work; to get tasks done through the hands of others.

His father-in-law was correcting him. The younger man had the position as the singular leader of an immense organization. He was a brilliant administrator and was universally respected as a wise decision-maker. And he did it all.

He worked nonstop from dawn to dusk. The elder counselor was concerned about his son-in-law's crushing burden. He was worried. The wise, old Jethro knew that his daughter's husband had to pace himself or his health would suffer.

Moses was facing the common management challenge of the ages, "If you want something done right you've got to do it yourself."

This traditional "management" maxim is, of course, a lie.

If the manager does the doing, he's not performing as a manager—he's backsliding to staffer. The manager is doing the literal hands-on work that individual contributors should be doing (even if the staff is doing the job badly).

The manager does no "work" as commonly understood by non-managers. The boss does not roll up his sleeves and get his hands dirty. Sure, there are exceptions, but "hands-on" micromanagement was the rule for Moses the ruler.

Managers just don't get things done. Macro-management gets things done through the active, thinking support of other people. Jethro advised Moses on this management fundamental of the ages: find talented, faithful men who will act in your stead.

> *When his father-in-law saw all that Moses was doing for the people, he said, "What is this you are doing for the people? Why do you alone sit as judge, while all these people stand around you from morning till evening?"*
>
> *Moses answered him, "Because the people come to me to seek God's will. Whenever they have a dispute, it is brought to me, and I decide between the parties and inform them of God's decrees and instructions."*
>
> *Moses' father-in-law replied, "What you are doing is not good. You and these people who come to you will only wear yourselves out. The work is too heavy for you; you cannot handle it alone.*
>
> *Listen now to me and I will give you some advice, and may God be with you. You must be the people's representative before God and bring their disputes to him. Teach them his decrees and instructions, and show them the way they are to live and how they are to behave.*
>
> *But select capable men from all the people—men who fear God, trustworthy men who hate dishonest gain—and appoint them as officials over thousands, hundreds, fifties and tens. Have them serve as judges for*

the people at all times, but have them bring every difficult case to you; the simple cases they can decide themselves. That will make your load lighter, because they will share it with you. If you do this and God so commands, you will be able to stand the strain, and all these people will go home satisfied."

Moses listened to his father-in-law and did everything he said.

Moses listened. The Israelites had a new hierarchal organization that any manager today would see as the familiar pyramid org chart. The new structure enabled Moses to lead his people out of the desert wilderness to the Promised Land.

The success was possible because Moses followed the advice of his father-in-law and learned to delegate.

Exodus 18:21b, says to find competent men and *appoint them as officials over thousands, hundreds, fifties and tens.* Delegate. Enable Followership.

Law *vs.* Grace: do as I want; not as I say.

Every manager comes to work each morning with a secret that he will share with no one in his organization. Which is, his direct reports terrify him. Maybe not like the apocryphal concern General Patton had. In the movie bearing his name, the general said of his men, *They'll lose their fear of the Germans. I only hope to God they never lose their fear of me...*

Because even the most battle-hardened manager has two great fears:

The staffer *will not do* exactly as he is told, and,

The staffer *will do* exactly as he is told.

Bum Phillips, the former coach of the Houston Oilers, once said that "There are two kinds of football players ain't worth a [darn]: the one that never does what he's told, and the other that never does anything *except* what he's told." (Nelson 2003)

But the manager wants both to be obeyed and to have the work done right, even if the management process is flawed. It's a conundrum—coordinating the boss-compliance and rule-breaking initiative at exactly the right time.

How can the manager ever get things done?

There must be obedience in an organization. A group of individuals without a ranking structure of authority and followership is not an organization—it is a mob.

Avoiding mob-rule and getting compliance in following directions comes in three flavors:

A. Incompetent
B. Vicious
C. Delightful

To begin, even the novice manager can recognize Incompetent/ Non-Compliance (A).

Or the leader can rejoice when staff follows directions and produces an amazing outcome (C). This is simple Moses law-giving and law obeying.

But life (and management) is not so simple.

Every boss knows the power that the staffer has in doing exactly what was directed. "If the Boss wants it really bad," Vicious Compliance (B) says, "how do we give it to him?"

"Really bad…"

The support staff and direct reports can do exactly as requested and still make the boss look silly.

The story is told of a new Army doctor, not well liked. The obnoxious physician requested 1,000 tongue depressors. The staff exchanged sideways glances and placed the order.

When a thousand boxes of tongue depressors were crated in, the doctor exploded, "You idiots! I only wanted a 1,000—not a 1,000 boxes."

The staff didn't bother to tell him the unit of measure was by the box and not by the individual item. The team did precisely as instructed. But they should have protected the boss from his own ignorance.

Hence the manager needs mercy and grace.

Mercy is not getting a punishment we may deserve (B). Grace is getting a reward we may not deserve (C).

Grace provides the margin that propels excellent organizations to high achievement. The manager should extend mercy to the repentant, viciously compliant staffer. Keeping in mind that he wants to stimulate initiative—focusing on the batting average, not the individual swing. But the manager himself also needs mercy and grace, because, unlike Jesus, the manager will be often wrong too.

Or worse. The manager's staff may detest him like our Army doctor. The staffers could also be so terrified that they are unable to initiate anything; they are only doing what they are told.

The physician and staff both need help. Each failed to manage the relationship. But the team can be made to be effective with training. And with mercy, grace, and truth.

For the law was given through Moses; grace and truth came through Jesus Christ. *John 1:17.*

What does *U-nO-Dir* look like in real-life application? It's a quick email, text, or voice message that says: Unless Otherwise Directed, I will move on this action. I will commence fire. Then the staffer-as-adult moves forward, with the safety net that if he has miscalculated—or had imperfect information—the manager still has opportunity for intervention.

How does the staffer get to the status of "unless otherwise directed?" How does the manager groom his staff to assume the trusted position of acting *U-nO-Dir*?

This exalted situation is achieved on a simple, three-step growing process from child to teenager to adulthood.

Child. This is an attitude not an age. Your manager may "mother" his team at work, but let's not make the supervisor a nanny. Every parent can attest to the two bothersome child-challenges: noise or, worse, silence.

The silent child or invisible staffer is a concern both for manager and parent. If the adult-leader cannot hear anything, the worry is, is the child safe? Is the staffer working? If the parent-boss hears nothing and aware of only silence, the manager-mom gets nervous. A panicky superior is never good.

If the manager hears too little from his children, he could also hear too much. This is where the child complains to a parent, "I'm bored." The staffer-as-child asks, "What do I do? What do I do?" Nonstop, forever asking for direction. Maybe the staffer is compliant, maybe not—but the child takes no initiative. *Completed Staff Work* demands thinking and anticipation. Your manager may have children at home; he doesn't need any at work.

What can the manager do? Forbid childhood. The childless manager must have two policies. First, the staffer only comes to the manager with a recommendation, an action, or an idea.

And second, the staffer is not permitted to ask what to do. The manager demands options. This will accelerate childhood to teenager.

The staffer can help his manager and avoid acting the child. Remember, in any kind of downturn the "children" are the first to be fired.

Teen. After the manager bans the babies, the maturing staffer and manager grow together. Like any good teenager-parent relationship, limits are tested. The employee as teen will exercise initiative and ideas and anticipates next moves. The boss-as-parent-figure now expects advice and wants the staffer to execute the recommendation.

But the teen may not be there yet. The manager looks for the staffer to discover the opportunity or problem, research options, and make a proposal. But what parent trusts every teenager's action? The solution for management, as in parenting, is a simple control measure: have the young adult ask first. Take action on a request only on approval. Not all 16-year-olds might be allowed to take dad's keys and run off in the Mercedes. As the teen grows, the boss will consider allowing the staffer to develop a course of action—then implement and alert the manager afterwards. This is grown-up "empowerment."

Adult. This final stage is earned and not given. To be treated as an adult is to permit the employee to take action without notifying the manager beforehand. This mature staffer foresees what his supervisor would do, then does it. This is a risk for the manager. The adult-in-training is going to make mistakes. Indeed, if he is not making mistakes, he is not being pushed hard enough. This is the terror for the manager-as-parent: the student-driver growing into an adult decision-maker might dent a fender.

Here the wisdom and judgment of the manager is applied. The boss needs to motivate and train his team and still meet company goals. The staffer needs to experience bending without breaking, without hurting the organization.

Where are the lines and guidelines?

Each learning task depends on the situation, the staffer and the manager. Is the boss also learning and inexperienced? Is the staffer competent? Does the situation allow for acceptable risk? The manager makes this determination on this multi-variable challenge. This is why managers earn and deserve outsized compensation.

The best managers develop subordinates who act as trusted subordinates. Tasks are easily delegated to adults. The best staffers push for this training. This is hard work.

U-nO-Dir: an acronym for "Unless Otherwise Directed." This is a freedom given by the superior and earned by the subordinate to act in the manager's name. It says that the staffer will act unless his boss tells him to stop. It is permission to do what the boss would do if he had time. This is the nirvana for the Alert Staffer where he has become the representative-deputy to his manager.

Discussion Questions
1. How is *U-nO-Dir* status earned?
2. How is delegation earned?
3. Why are "children" the first to be terminated in a budget cut?
4. Teens should be tested. Why?
5. Adulthood is risky. What is the benefit?

CHAPTER 26

Value: The one word that describes marketing and usefulness.

VALUE IS THE COMPELLING WORTH of a staff recommendation or a management decision where no one needs to "think it over." The action is so obvious that contentious debate may not be necessary.

The assessment/appeal/importance is determined not by the seller/presenter, but by the buyer.

Eject Eject Eject. [3] It is your career responsibility to be valuable or get out of the boat.

The athlete had been training for years for this competition. Then he jumped ship. The crew was rowing their thin shell in a race and the team was pulling hard on the oars.

Then an oar breaks.

---

3   Command issued by a jet pilot to leave an aircraft in flight. *Eject Eject Eject* There is a one-in-three chance of a broken back caused by the explosive force of blowing the seat and pilot out of the jet. The odds of the alternative—death—are 100 percent. The better option is to vacate the venue.

In the days of yore, an oar was made of wood and would bend and break; the broken oar would be fished from the water and proudly displayed as a trophy by the oar-breaking oarsman.

Oars break less today due to their nearly indestructible composite material. But they still crack occasionally and ejecting is in the back of every competitor's mind. An oarsman minus his oar is deadweight slowing the shell.

Time to jump ship.

Spectators along the banks of the regatta's course have been known to break out and cheer for the man who jumps overboard.

Every person will reach a point in his or her career when there will not be a fit between the skills demanded by the job and the value the employee can deliver. The answer to this question is marked-off in another race between the employee and his manager: Who will notice first?

The employee should.

Legendary violinist Jascha Heifetz said, "The discipline of practice every day is essential. When I skip a day, I notice a difference in my playing. After two days, the critics notice, and after three days, so does the audience."

It is best if the individual discovers his shortcomings before his manager. The self-aware worker will notice—better notice—before anyone else that there are some tasks beyond his current expertise. The worker should either get the needed training or move to another job in the company.

But if no fit is found, then be prepared to jump ship before you are thrown overboard. Leave on your own terms.

As Jack Welch would say, "Don't be a victim." Be in control of your own career. Remember, it is not the person, not the employee who is rejected, but his *work*. Leave and jump ship before you are fired.

If anyone will not welcome you or listen to your words, leave that home or town and shake the dust off your feet. Matthew 10:14

★

The Alert Student in *Completed Staff Work* is constantly asking himself and those around him, "How are we adding value?"

That reply had better come fast and easy. If you are confused or doubtful, don't expect your boss, peers, or direct reports to answer for you.

The response template is simple. Our value to the organization is quantified by one or more of these feature-descriptors:

- Faster
- Better
- Cheaper

These superlatives match with your personal advantages of:

- Time
- Talent
- Treasure

And overlay with the organization's constraints of:

- Deadlines
- Human Resources
- Budget

Our value is helping meet company goals. We are a benefit to the boss.

The value of your performance is, of course, different from your value as a person. We are all equal in the eyes of the Creator. But performance will vary from person to person. Our job is to sell the value of our organization through our work.

The demonstrated advantage of a person's work starts during the hiring process.

★

Futurist A track record shows value and the lane travelled and the likely path ahead.

Your Business Professor was conducting another interview with a terrific job applicant in the private sector. I knew the candidate was wonderful because he told me so. He promised me all of the amazing work he was going to do. (I always note the verb tense used.)

He rattled on and on about what he could do for me in the future. The job seeker might have been half right.

But I didn't hire half of him. I hired zero of him.

The half I liked was his optimism about future performance. That was a start. Every manager hires an employee on the hope, prayer, and promise that the added head-count will be a value add. But how would I know?

Every hiring manager is a fortuneteller attempting to predict what a candidate will do in the future. There is only one way to foretell what will happen tomorrow. It is by a careful review of what happened yesterday. The best indicator of future performance is past performance.

The manager is a futurist using pattern recognition. Smart hiring and decision-making for the future involves looking backward. No one really knows how any one person will work out. We cannot eliminate future risk. But we can minimize our exposure to failure.

I am placing a bet on the person I hire. And, as a condition of continued (managerial) employment, I better have more wins than losses. When I make a wager on a candidate, I need to evaluate his past behavior. I look for some indication that success is a way of life. This is not a subjective measure. What I need to be able to see—and every job seeker should show—is measurable performance.

Numbers, numbers, numbers.

In this current egalitarian age, every entry-level employee grows up collecting participation trophies. This is when every kid on the team gets an award, whether or not he deserves it. No one's feelings get hurt. Goodness, in some leagues they don't even keep score.

But real management keeps score using real numbers. Fuzzy mathematicians need not apply. Realized revenue is not counted in good intentions or desire. It is not enough just to have been on the winning team. I'm not hiring the whole team.

In any job interview, tell me how you affected the score. What were your sales numbers? Numbers of transactions processed? Number of defects reduced? What went up? What went down? Give me a number. Show me your W-2. If nothing else, you cite perfect attendance on the job, never taking a sick day.

That might be a zero I would hire.

And my honesty will testify for me in the future, whenever you check on the wages you have paid me. Genesis 30:33

We want to have something to show for our efforts. But the hardest work is sometimes playing defense where nothing happens. You are problem-solving that may not advance an agenda. Sometimes the "better" cannot be seen.

Focus If it's not core, then it's going offshore.

Your Business Professor was struggling to manage my part of a $200-million-dollar project at an All-Staff Meeting. There were whispers between my directors and some of their backbenching assistants. Something was odd about their conversations. Their language was off-kilter.

In hushed tones I heard, *client specs...* I stopped and thought.

"If your paycheck does not have my company's name on it," I ask, "please indicate by raising your hand."

Two-thirds of my "team" members were outside consultants.

I got mad without a good reason. I wanted complete control of everything, everywhere.

I was, of course, an amateur manager. But I would learn. I would become an (out)sourcer's apprentice. Some parts of my business deserved more of my immediate attention than others.

The story is told of Jack Welch, former GE CEO as he speaks of the difference between the "support" and "core" parts of a business,

> *In the late 1980s, during a period of intense competitive ferment, [Peter] Drucker was summoned back to GE...*
>
> *"Make sure that your back room is their front room," recalls Welch. It was a statement that helped define Welch's approach to a wave of outsourcing.*
>
> *"In other words, don't you do guard services at your plant. Get someone who specializes in guard services" to do them for you. Get rid of in-house printing, in-house conferences services, and any business than isn't the core of your focus."*
>
> *Explains Welch, "[Drucker] made it very clear what a waste" it was to be in marginal activities where, inevitably, GE would put its "weakest people." (Gabor 2000)*

How does the Alert Staffer and manager determine the difference between the core of a business from the merely critical-support component?

The core of any going concern is what the customer walks away with after crashing into your company. Support functions assist the core.

Always work in the core of a business—where the *value* is. For example, if your passion is lawn care maintenance then work in, say, a landscape business. Do not work in grounds maintenance at an accounting firm.

If your passion is bookkeeping, work at a bookkeeping firm. Do not do the back-office bookkeeping at a lawn care company.

Core for one company is support at another.

Support at one company is core for another.

The focused CEO cares about core because that is of primary importance and the value to the customer. Critical-support work is an unfocused blur.

Entrepreneur Richard Koch writes,

> *Unless we have numbers or 80/20 Thinking to guide us, most things always appear more important than the few things that are actually more important.*
>
> *Even if we accept the point in our minds, it is difficult to make the next hop to focused action. Keep the "vital few" in the forefront of your brain. And keep reviewing whether you are spending more time and effort on the vital few rather than the trivial many. (Koch 1999)*

I learned this the hard way.

My project team was a majority of outsourced talent and these consultants were then doing their own outsourcing. Seamlessly (to me) the consulting firms were sub-subcontracting downstream to the Indian subcontinent. It was faster, better, cheaper, and all that.

I stopped my madness. I was getting my core needs met. The customers were delighted. The consultants and all that noncore, critical-support stuff was getting done in other time zones.

I didn't need to be everywhere.

Value can be seen when the decision maker does not need "to think it over." The boss trusts the content of your recommendation and your character and your track record. This means that the sign-off decision process can be sped up because the manager does not need to agonize over the input from you, the value-added staffer.

Discussion Questions
1. What is "value?"
2. Who determines value? The seller or buyer? Why?
3. How is value added?
4. Jack Welch says, "Never be a victim." Explain.
5. Managers want "measurable performance." Discuss.
6. What is the difference between core and support units?
7. Is "outsourcing" an evil? Explain.
8. Why would the boss not need to "think it over?"
9. How can a manager predict future performance?

CHAPTER 27

Credit: Be in everyone's debt; owe everyone, gratefully.

GIVE RECOGNITION: IT IS BETTER to give and give (with the humility of a servant's heart) than to receive. *And whoever wants to be first must be slave of all.* Mark 10:44

Ronald Reagan believed that, "There is no limit to what a man can do or where he can go if he doesn't mind who gets the credit." He had a plaque with the quote sitting on his desk in the Oval Office.

Happiness can follow when personal goals serve other people. Managers at the top of the org chart should be the true servant-leaders noted in the good news of the Gospels.

So how does the manager get started?

The leader must look at presenting her long-term vision, indeed every communication, as a sales transaction: Someone is buying and someone is selling. The best sales professionals and the best CEOs know that the best deals are made when the other party is made happy.

Win-win negotiating and all that.

What is the first thing the wanna-be-boss can practice to be the servant of all?

The easiest way is to buy servant-hood. No, that can't be purchased with cash—but with organizational capital. That is to say: *give credit.*

Giving credit to others is a form of servant-hood. It's a way of selling yourself as leader of the team. Receiving recognition creates happiness in both buyer and seller. Being the "slave" to your staff, peers, and manager is the best path toward getting profitable buy-in for your recommendations.

In Chapter 14 we learned that Basketball Hall of Famer, University of North Carolina Tar Heels coach Dean Smith focused on process. But the man who was known as the "gentleman and coach" also emphasized sharing credit:

> *...I wanted tangible evidence that North Carolina's players and coaches recognized and appreciated a good pass that led to a basket. UCLA's coaching great John Wooden and I talked about it far back as the mid-1960s, when he said he wanted the recipient of a pass that led to a basket to say thank you to the passer or wink at him.*
>
> *That was a good idea, but I wanted a stronger, more visible signal of thanks. I preferred a gesture that the fans could see. The media too. So we asked the player who scored to point to the man who gave him the pass that resulted in the basket, to show appreciation for an unselfish act that helped the team...Thank the passer by pointing to him...It became contagious... (Smith 2004)*

The presidential-servant keeps nothing—not even credit. Give it away.

Historian Gordon S. Wood, winner of the Pulitzer Prize, explains this credit-debt doctrine in *The Americanization of Benjamin*

Franklin (2004), where Franklin, "[W]on his superiors over by allowing them to patronize him."

When one member of the legislature, a gentleman of fortune and education, opposed his election as clerk of the assembly, Franklin made him his friend by borrowing a book from him, thus, he would say, demonstrating the truth of an old maxim [from Franklin's *Autobiography*], *He that has once done you a Kindness will be more ready to do you another, than he who you yourself have obliged...*

Wood points out that this credit *vs* debt also moves in the reverse direction,

> *Franklin believed that if a post were offered him he could not turn it down. "It would be a terrible mistake, he told his son, "to decline any favour so great a man expressed an inclination to do me, because at court if one shews an unwillingness to be obliged it is often construed as a mark of mental hostility, and one makes an enemy."*

Our lesson today is to never turn down a favor, be it great or small. For example, if you are presented with the smallest kindness, such as coffee offered by a receptionist—always accept. Graciously. Even if you have to pour it into a plant later.

Indebted? When is being in debt a joyful experience?

There is another source of power and pain that can be used to make a smoothly running organization: the exchange of personal favors.

Many people think, and practice, a variation of this myth: "Make a person think he owes you something; if he is indebted to you he will appreciate you—if he owes you, he will be grateful to you."

This is, of course, a misunderstanding of human nature. It is also how the amateur believes power is wielded. The experienced professional knows better. As the Bible says, ...*the borrower is slave to the lender,* Proverbs 22:7b

For instance, a bank "gives" you a loan. You repay the loan over 36 months. You do not love your banker.

You hate him for each and every month of the term of the loan. Whatever people may believe in the logic of the loan, no one enjoys being in debt.

The only time death is popular is when the last payment is made on the house. "Mortgage" has as its root word the French word for "dead"—*mort.* Even a church, when the building is finally paid off, will burn the mortgage.

If we hate the bank, we also hate the banker. The banker has power over us; he owns a piece of our soul. So if there is so much influence in this transaction how can we become Power Brokers for good?

General George Marshall gives us an example of how to work "debt" to the manager's advantage. Marshall was described by Winston Churchill as the "Organizer of Victory." Marshall's biographer, Leonard Mosley, used the accolade for his book. Marshall was the U.S. Army's top military leader during World War II and was the all-powerful decision-maker on key leadership positions.

The four verbs of management provide the foundation for everything else: plan, organize, lead, and control. To organize is to determine what human resources will be placed into what capacity. ("Human resources" is business-speak for "people.")

Marshall also knew how to motivate as a part of the leadership of people. He well understood the strange, fickle nature of the human condition: If I perform a favor for you, you may or may not be grateful. But you would be much obliged to me much as if I were a banker making a loan to you. This is the root of obligation. And no one wants to be obligated to anyone. General Marshall said,

If you want a man to be for you never let him feel he is dependent on you. Because he is not going to like you at all. If you really want to have the guy be for you, find some way to make him feel you are in some way dependent on him. (Mosley 1982)

Even though Marshall controlled the careers and promotions of thousands of senior officers, he was careful to make sure that the appreciation flowed from the top down. [4]

(Researchers have discussed a "Little Black Book" where Marshall kept track of the men he was grooming for promotion. One can only imagine the terror—and motivation—that even the rumored existence of such a record would create.)

Debt management is counterintuitive. People will love you when they do things *for* you. Not for what they get *from* you. Odd. So how does the novice manager practice the art of getting favors done for them—so that the received generosity will be appreciated?

The professional will look for anything, however microscopic, for which to thank someone. The pro is always grateful and expresses the indebtedness. It would also have the added benefit of being true. Find and acknowledge the good that another has done for you—even if inadvertent—and express appreciation.

The next time someone does the slightest kindness, the slightest head fake of civility, thank him or her.

In another more refined generation in previous centuries, men and women of letters would close a correspondence with something like, *Your Obedient Servant* or *Your Humble Servant*. This was the fashion then.

It was the duty of nobility to be gracious and tolerant. *Noblesse oblige*. Today the thoughtful manager might close every email and every letter with one of the following:

---

4   Today it is customary to greet anyone who served in uniform with the salutation, "Thank you for your service…"

I owe you,
We remain in your debt,
I am much obliged,

This is debt accumulation and appreciation that makes everyone feel better.

What is a common rate of rejection -- and of return? How many favors must the manager give for each favor received?

"About 10 percent." This is the answer that comes back in nearly every seminar. In sales training classes, we review the ratio of referrals given out to the number received. The estimates are always revealing and disturbing.

It is 10:1.

The sales professionals will complain that for every ten leads for new business that they will forward to other sales representatives they will get one lead back. Give ten out; get one back. "It is not fair," clients say.

"You are right," I reply. "It is not fair, few things in life are—especially in sales and sales referrals, but we must decide to be proactive; to be in control of the events that affect our work—even if the returns are marginal."

"It seems that we should get more appreciation...more love...?" The class asks with one voice.

"So it would appear," I say, and then pause.

"How many lepers did Jesus heal as recorded in chapter 17 of Luke?"

Ten, the Bible students in the audience answer.

The question follows to challenge them, "And how many came back to Jesus to thank him?"

The class is still for a few seconds and one person replies softly, "one."

Now if the Creator of the universe—who worked the miracle of healing leprosy—can only get a 10 percent response rate, what makes you think—you mere mortal—that you could do better than Jesus?

> *Jesus asked, "Were not all ten cleansed? Where are the other nine?*
> Luke 17:17

It is not recorded if the nine cured lepers were among the mockers at Christ's crucifixion, but who would be surprised if they were? The fallen nature of the human condition is like that.

And hasn't gotten much better in two millennia. But good, God-fearing citizens try to be generous and continue to give even if the gift is not recognized.

This is the American way: to "give something back."

In the 1830s Frenchman Alexis de Tocqueville traveled across the young America to explore and document why America was so successful—what has come to be called "American Exceptionalism." In part, the new USA was acting out the "good of giving" that Jesus did. And Americans did not expect the thanks of the receiver—or even payment—or even reciprocal consideration.

Tocqueville wrote in *Democracy in America*, in 1836, that Americans demonstrated "enlightened self-interest" with something he called "self-interest rightly understood,"

The Americans, on the contrary, are fond of explaining almost all the actions of their lives by the principle of interest rightly understood; they show with complacency how an enlightened regard for themselves constantly prompts them to assist each other, and inclines them willingly to sacrifice a portion of their time and property to the welfare of the state.

Two centuries later, this concept of enlightened self-interest is still firmly embedded in the American subconscious. Tocqueville would have recognized the 2000 movie *Pay It Forward* starring Kevin Spacey and Helen Hunt. In the movie, a teacher challenges his class to change the world by helping other people without expecting anything in return. It changes the life of one of his students, and becomes a Pay It Forward movement. A uniquely American movement.

Americans were (are) not naïve. The European Tocqueville learned that Americans giving and getting was not a lateral, binary, two-way transaction. Giving was done in a loop where the favor would circle back to the originator from a different direction. But the favor was returned.

Whenever there was a barn raising, the owner would benefit and would eventually return the favor directly or indirectly to the person or to someone else in the community. This was done without keeping records, without intrusive government. Still today, radio stations regularly run Pay It Forward days when Americans going through fast-food drive-thru lines buy the meal, or the coffee, for the drivers behind them. It creates a debt. Pass it on. Pay it forward.

How does this work in management? Create an atmosphere of generosity. Morton Blackwell, founder of the Leadership Institute says, "A stable movement requires a healthy, reciprocal I.O.U. flow among its participants. Don't keep a careful tally."

Decide to do the favor and expect nothing in return. Goodwill will still return to you.

★

Feel-good movies like *Pay It Forward* may be overly earnest. But this concept of personal indebtedness is deeply serious for the manager/leader, with real-world consequence. Author Colleen McCullough notes in her historical novels where Caesar is owed a debt of gratitude, "I want those I pardon to resume their positions in Rome..." Why did the all-powerful dictator do this? To, "give me a few challenges...I truly cannot bear the thought of being surrounded by sycophants!"

This might work—until the long knives come out in mid-March. No one wants to be in debt.

Credit: is to be in everyone's debt. This sounds strange and counterintuitive but it works in the doctrine of *Completed Staff Work*. Everyone likes to be owed. No one likes to be in debt. Not to a bank or to another person. We would rather have others owe us, rather than to owe others. Everyone wants to be in a "superior" position. An Accounts Receivable is preferred over an Accounts Payable. However, we can sell easier if the perception is that we "owe" the client/manager or coworker. No one must ever feel that that they owe us.

Discussion Questions
1. Why is it better to give than to receive?
2. What did Ronald Reagan say about credit?
3. *And whoever wants to be first must be slave of all*, Mark 10:44. Explain.
4. Why are Big Banks and loan sharks hated?
5. I will appreciate you when I can help you. Why?
6. What is the ratio of favors given to favors received? Give an example.
7. What is "self-interest, rightly understood?"

CHAPTER 28

Loyal: Do the work as if the decision had been yours.

Therefore, since we are surrounded by such a great cloud of witnesses, let us throw off everything that hinders and the sin that so easily entangles... Hebrews 12:1a

EVERY NEW CEO NEEDS A loyal team to begin his job; he needs a clean sweep.

The young CEO was following in the footsteps of a legend and was concerned about making too many changes too soon.

Or so he said.

I advised him to clean house and replace key senior managers with his own lineup. He was hired by the board of directors to take the company in a new direction. He would need to be surrounded by his own team.

He said, "I need to give these personnel decisions some careful thought..." A diplomatic backing-out that communicated *I don't know...maybe later.*

Actually, I found out that he didn't like to fire people. Nobody does.

He knew political history and he said that he was hoping for a seamless transition. There are some examples of such transitions in the nation's highest office.

After John F. Kennedy was assassinated in 1963, his Vice President Lyndon B. Johnson retained most of Kennedy's cabinet appointees for continuity. Kennedy and Johnson had similar agendas and their philosophies were aligned. And LBJ, who had been the former Senate Majority Leader, could make things happen on the force of his oversized Texas personality.

Eleven years later in 1974, vice president Gerald Ford would keep Nixon's staff as well. After Nixon resigned as a result of the Watergate scandal and cover-up, the appointed president Ford was concerned about the aftershocks. Ford was more anxious about calming the country than running it. Ford's then chief of staff, Donald Rumsfeld, wrote (2013), "He opted for conformity over change...he was uncomfortable having to tell people who had served loyally that they would have to leave."

Rumsfeld advises senior leaders to assemble an entourage of like-minded team managers and bring the crew with them. "Build your own—and do it fast...You will benefit and those departing will know they are not leaving because of poor performance..."

The CEO whom Your Business Professor was counseling was slow to bring on new talent. His new initiatives were implemented even slower. Time could have been saved with his own team.

The origin of loyalty is from the Old French "*loialte*." The common root is from the Latin word for law. (Wikipedia 2017) Loyalty should be as compelling as law.

★

A friend loves at all times, and a brother is born for a time of adversity. Proverbs 17:17

What does loyalty look like? As Morton Blackwell writes in "The Laws of the Public Policy Process," *Don't fully trust anyone until he has stuck with a good cause which he saw was losing.* Be a friend; stand by your man to get things done.

"I don't believe it." As the story goes, mayor William Donald Schaefer (1921 to 2011) just heard a terrible, irrefutable truth about a friend. Reporters pressed him on the obvious evidence of a scandalous misdeed of a member of the Baltimore politico's inner circle. Schaefer instantly and emphatically stood with his friend.

He *would not hear of it;* the politician *dismissed the accusation out of hand.* The reporters confronted Schaefer; the mayor pushed back, *I just don't believe it.* The journalists stopped when they got the story: it wasn't the alleged misdeed of a staffer. It was the loyalty of a friend.

The mayor of Baltimore was a public servant for some 50 years. In the mid-1980s Schaefer also served as Maryland's governor (perhaps simultaneously—it was hard to tell).

He understood loyalty. He trusted and was trusted. This was how he got things done.

The staffer must understand that his manager will not always seem to make the right decision. Even after considering all the options and recommendations, the boss will make an "odd" decision. Sometimes there won't be time to explain the direction.

Or, more likely, the boss can't share confidential background information or the timing is wrong.

Or the supervisor is still learning management-on-the-job and the thousands of variables to weigh. And sometimes the CEO just gets it wrong. How can the staffer manage his manager in this situation?

A team of professionals can take most any unusual decision and deliver the desired outcome. If senior management falters on those plan-organize-lead-control skills, the skilled subordinate managers and staff can still accomplish the task through execution.

This is how loyalty can help the mission to succeed. The team will adopt and implement the senior manager's determination as if the decision were their own.

This assumes that the choices and execution are legal. Of course, perhaps that can be a dangerous assumption in business, or in Louisiana politics.

The story is told of Governor Earl K. Long (1895 to 1960) of The Bayou State who was counseling one of his staffers. The smug young aide says, "I'm with you when you're right. But not when you're wrong."

Governor Long snaps, "You stupid son of a b!tch. I don't need you when I'm right."

The aide should have been more concerned that right and wrong meant legal and illegal. Our actions in loyal *Completed Staff Work* remain within the law. But inside that boundary, let's remember Imperfection from Chapter 11—.300 is a good batting average. Even among the most scrupulously principled managers, not every decision will be right or correct.

That's why, as Long knew, few things are more valuable than a faithful friend.

Morton Blackwell, founder of the Leadership Institute, offers another face of the political from Louisiana. He is direct and ethical, "In politics, [office or otherwise] you have your word and your friends; go back on either and you're dead."

★

Stay there, eating and drinking whatever they give you, for the worker deserves his wages. Do not move around from house to house.
Luke 10:7

If you want a friend while in management, get a dog. [5]

The CEO was in a funk. His top scientist had just given notice and was leaving for another company in a different industry.

"What did we do wrong?" the boss asked. "Why did he leave?"

"Did he get a better offer?" I asked.

"Yes," the boss sighed. "Almost double."

"Goodness," I said. "Now—I know you wouldn't leave if offered twice the money…" The CEO is looking down, silent and sad.

Academia, consultants, and journalists give us nonstop happy talk about how We Are All Family. Until another person buys the love and loyalty.

You are not married to your job. You are not an indentured servant.

Your staffers are rented relationships. It is less a marriage than it is some other temporary transaction.

Frederick Herzberg was a psychologist who served a tour of duty in the Army. He earned a doctorate focusing on electronic shock therapy. His unusual background and research helps us understand how people behave in organizations.

---

5   The earliest evidence for this family of quotes comes from a marketing campaign, a 1911 American newspaper advertisement in the "Pets for Sale" section advised: "If you want a friend—buy a dog!" (Crye 2013)

"If you want a friend in Washington, get a dog," is often misattributed to Harry Truman while he was president in Washington, D.C. He never owned a dog.

The old Armed Forces joke cannot be attributed to him,
Question: "Why are you banging your head against that wall?"
Answer: "Because it feels so good when I stop…"
(Mega)Herz-berg found that "stopping the bad" is as important
as "doing the good."
We learn that Herzberg in the late 1950s,

> *[W]as surprised to find that feeling good and feeling bad resulted from entirely different sets of factors; that is, low pay may have made a particular person feel bad, but it was not high pay that had made that person feel good.*

Instead, Herzberg discovered that there are completely different issues involved,

> *[C]alled hygiene factors…causing dissatisfaction are supervision, working conditions, interpersonal relations, pay, job security, company policies, and administration.*

Hygiene is necessary at work as in any dating relationship. Sweet perfume may not make a person attractive, but horrible body odor can make a person unattractive.

Good hygiene is noticeable in its absence. And this is why these factors are difficult to manage. An employee must be paid enough to satisfy his perceived basic needs: clean enough restrooms, a comfortable enough office chair, and about enough money.

The minimum "enough" is always changing. It is the manager's job to know when enough is enough. In the for-profit business world people work for a reason. The "why" people work is a motivator—but we can only work to change the world if we can pay the rent. (Blackwell) We need something in exchange for our labors. That's why it's called "consideration."

Every thoughtful business relationship requires loyalty and compensation.

Your Business Professor defines management as being in a relationship. A reciprocal one. No one works for free. And the bonds of loyalty should not substitute for the requirements of human dignity.

Loyalty is what every manager craves for in a smoothly running business unit. The boss understands that staffer faithfulness can reduce risk in decision-making. Loyal peers and direct reports can have the manager's and the organization's best interest at heart. You, the loyal staffer, will execute a task as if the manager's decision had been yours.

Discussion Questions
1. What is loyalty in business?
2. Why should a new manager bring on his own staffers?
3. Loyalty has origins rooted in law. Discuss.
4. How can we spot loyalty?
5. When does loyalty stop?
6. How does loyalty produce *Completed Staff Work*?

REFERENCES AND
NOTES

YES, READ THEM. THERE WILL be a citation here of an expert who will change your life and thinking as mine has changed. Let me know who.

INTRODUCTION

"...**For I myself am a man under authority, with soldiers under me**." From the book of Matthew 8:9.

"**A Roman who had *auctoritas* could get things done without ever having to give a direct order...**" Steve Forbes and John Prevas, *Power Ambition Glory: The Stunning Parallels Between Great Leaders of the Ancient World and Today...and the Lessons You Can Learn* (New York: Three Rivers Press, 2010), 265.

"**Management by Walking Around**" was made popular by management consultants Tom Peters and Robert H. Waterman, Wikipedia, https://en.wikipedia.org/wiki/Management_by_wandering_around accessed 6 May 2017.

"**It is finished**." Christ's last words on the Cross from the book of John 19:30.

CHAPTER 1, ANTICIPATION

"Completed Staff Work" There are references, some dated, some not, to this phrase. But Archer L. Lerch has the earliest citation as of this writing. See http://www.yoest.com/wp-content/uploads/2015/12/Completed-Staff-Work-article.pdf accessed 15 May 2017.

"The Memo" Classified RESTRICTED from General MacArthur's staff is undated but there is strong evidence that it might pre-date Lerch's. More research is needed. See The Memo: http://www.yoest.com/2016/12/31/the-memo-leadership-and-followership-in-completed-staff-work/ accessed 15 May 2017.

CHAPTER 2, DECISION

"One must be a good butcher" Eliot A. Cohen, *Supreme Command: Soldiers, Statesmen and Leadership in Wartime* (New York, NY: The Free Press, A division of Simon & Schuster, 2002), 215.

"...whereas master coaches focused on a smaller set of variables..." Scott Snook and Jeffrey T. Polzer write of this management challenge in a 2004 case study for *Harvard Business Review*, *The Army Crew Team*.

"A CEO does only three things." By Fred Wilson, AVC.com, August 2010 http://avc.com/2010/08/what-a-ceo-does/ accessed 6 May 2017.

"to make up one's mind" http://www.etymonline.com/index.php?term=decide accessed 6 May 2017.

"A good plan, violently executed now, is better than a perfect plan next week." Major General William A. Cohen, PhD, *The Art of the Strategist: 10 Essential Principles for Leading Your Company to Victory* (New York, NY: AMACOM, 2004), 53. Quoting General George Patton.

"Moltke (the elder) noted, a meticulously crafted operations plan does not survive contact with the enemy." Wikipedia *https://en.wikipedia.org/wiki/Helmuth_von_Moltke_the_Elder* accessed 6 May 2017.

"Little is worse than a manager who can't cut bait..." Jack Welch, *The Wall Street Journal,* "Four E's (a Jolly Good Fellow)," January 23, 2004. https://www.wsj.com/articles/ SB107481763013709619 accessed 6 May 2017.

"Courage is the first virtue that makes all other virtues possible." Travis Bradberry and Jean Greaves, *Leadership 2.0* (San Diego, CA: TalentSmart, 2012), 49. Quoting Aristotle.

"Every day, there were 15 things I could do..." D. Michael Lindsay, Ph.D. and M.G. Hager, *View From The Top: An Inside Look At How People In Power See And Shape The World* (Hoboken, NJ: Wiley, 2014), 58.

"Presidents make only tough decisions." Ibid 90.

CHAPTER 3, FINISHED

"Moses Men" Robert A. Caro, *The Power Broker: Robert Moses and the Fall of New York,* (New York, NY: Alfred A. Knopf, Inc., Distributed by Random House, 1974), 549.

"In that case, now I'll read it." *INTERVIEW WITH AMBASSADOR WINSTON LORD,* GWU.edu http:// nsarchive.gwu.edu/coldwar/interviews/episode-15/lord1. html accessed 6 May 2017.

"S.M.A.R.T. objectives..." Sharlyn Lauby, *The SMART Tool Human Resources Professionals Use Every Day,* **https://www. capella.edu/blogs/cublog/a-smart-tool-human- resource-management-professionals-use-daily/** accessed 6 May 2017, quoting Dr. George T. Doran.

"**Too Late**." William Manchester, *American Caesar: Douglas MacArthur 1880 – 1964* (New York, NY: Little, Brown and Company 1978), 82.

CHAPTER 4, DEPUTY

"**Evidently it did not matter whether I was there or not.**" Ernest Hemingway, *A Farewell to Arms* (New York, NY: Scribner, a division of Simon & Schuster, 1929) 14

"**Leadership…happens when you're not there.**" Ken Blanchard, *The Leadership Pill: The Missing Ingredient in Motivating People Today* (Free Press, a division of Simon & Schuster, 2003) 25.

"**common staff duties and responsibilities**" The US Army, *Commander And Staff Office Guide*, Army Tactics, Techniques, and Procedures, Number 5-0-1, Headquarters, Department of the Army, Washington, DC, (Books Express Publishing: 2011), 2-5

"**without requiring any serious intervention**" John H. Sununu, (2015-06-09). *The Quiet Man: The Indispensable Presidency of George H.W. Bush* (Kindle Location 2268). HarperCollins. Kindle Edition.

"**Seeing if Ike had sufficient ice in his veins…**" Thomas E. Ricks, *The Generals: American Military Command from World War II to Today* (New York, NY: Penguin Books, 2012) 56.

CHAPTER 5, AUTHORITY

"**Henri Fayol…published a book outlining 14 Principles of Management.**" Thomas S. Bateman, *et. al., Management* (New York, NY: McGraw-HIll/Irwin, 2013).

"**Scalar shares the Latin root for 'stairs' and 'scale' as to climb**" Wiktionary https://en.wiktionary.org/wiki/scale accessed 6 May 2017.

"divides the governance into three categories: Direct, Organizational and Strategic" Kevin Kruse, *The 3 Levels of Leadership Used by the US Army*, CEO.com, 11 June 2013 http://www.ceo.com/leadership_and_management/know-your-level-of-leadership/ accessed 6 May 2017.

"boundaryless" Jack Welch GE 2000 Annual Report http://www.ge.com/annual00/values/ accessed 6 May 2017.

"The best thing I did as a manager at PayPal" Peter Thiel and Blake Masters, (2014-09-16). *Zero to One: Notes on Startups, or How to Build the Future* (p. 123). Crown Publishing Group. Kindle Edition.

"Each mission requires only a single tactical action, and the commander employs tactics to accomplish each." US Army, United States Government (2012-01-19). Army Doctrine Publication ADP 3-0 (FM 3-0) Unified Land Operations October 2011 (pp. 9-10). Kindle Edition.

"achieve unity of effort" *Operations*, Army Doctrine Reference Publication, Number 3-0, The US Army, Headquarters, Department of the Army, Washington, DC, (2016), 1-5 http://www.apd.army.mil/epubs/DR_pubs/DR_a/pdf/web/ADRP%203-0%20FINAL%20WEB.pdf accessed 6 May 2017.

"I am a certified brake mechanic." The National Institute for Automotive Service Excellence (ASE) http://www.ase.com/Tests/ASE-Certification-Tests.aspx accessed 6 May 2017.

"The victorious Christian...is immortal..." Randolph O. Yeager, Ph.D., *The Renaissance New Testament*, Volume Fourteen, (Gretna, Louisiana: A Firebird Press Book, Pelican Publishing Company, 1983) 508.

CHAPTER 6, POWER
"I am determined to control events, not be controlled by them." President John Adams on the HBO series, "John Adams."

"different kinds of power" Mark Horstman, *The Effective Manager,* (Hoboken, NJ: Wiley, 2016) 107.

"*Git-R-Done*" Larry the Cable Guy http://www.larrythecableguy. com/ accessed 6 May 2017.

"Radar was the one who could get things done" Galina Espinoza, "Radar Check," *People Magazine,* August 9, 1999 http://people. com/archive/radar-check-vol-52-no-5/ accessed 6 May 2017.

"I memorized and then destroyed so as to become indispensable." Stephen P. Robbins and Timothy A. Judge, *Organizational Behavior* (Upper Saddle River, NJ: Prentice Hall, 2010) 425.

"Peter Drucker was...a unique genius." William A. Cohen, Ph.D., *Drucker on Marketing: Lessons from the World's Most Influential Business Thinker* (New York, NY: McGraw Hill Professional, 2012) 22.

"Jointness" Douglas J. Gillert, American Forces Press Service, 10 September 1996 http://archive.defense.gov/news/ newsarticle.aspx?id=40719 accessed 6 May 2017.

"Of all manifestations of power, restraint impresses men most." Powell, Colin; Koltz, Tony (2012-05-22). *It Worked for Me: In Life and Leadership* (Kindle Location 2728). Harper. Kindle Edition.

CHAPTER 7, FOLLOWERSHIP

"I would rather try to persuade a man to go along, because once I have persuaded him, he will stick..." Ethan M. Fishman, *el. al.* editors, *George Washington: Foundation of Presidential Leadership and Character* (Westport, CT: Praeger Publishers, an imprint of Greenwood Publishing Group, Inc., 2001) 85.

"By following" Ken Blanchard in *Christianity Today,* July 2007 http://www.christianitytoday.com/pastors/2007/july-online-only/day46.html accessed 7 May 2017.

"True greatness is found in the lowest, not the highest place." Randolph O. Yeager, Ph.D., *The Renaissance New Testament*, Volume Seven, (Gretna, Louisiana: A Firebird Press Book, Pelican Publishing Company, 1981) 214.

"Very Good" Peggy Noonan, *What I Saw at the Revolution: A Political Life in the Reagan Era* (New York, NY: Random House, LLC, 2003) 64.

"The best way to predict…a leader is to see what young people do at school." Henry Mintzberg, Bruce Ahlstrand, Joseph B. Lampel, *Management? It's not what you think!* (New York, NY: AMACOM, 2010) 106.

CHAPTER 8, EFFECTIVE

"The knowledge worker cannot be supervised closely or in detail." Peter F. Drucker, (2009-10-06). *The Effective Executive* (Harperbusiness Essentials) (p. 4). HarperCollins. Kindle Edition.

"People here are working on this on their own time." 'Gerber Will Make Formula for One Boy Who Needs It To Live,' *Los Angeles Times*, April 6, 1990 http://articles.latimes.com/1990-04-06/news/mn-667_1_gerber-make-formula accessed 7 May 7, 2017.

"I'm proud he was my son." 'Gerber Boy' *The Seattle Times*, January 26, 1995 http://community.seattletimes.nwsource.com/archive/?date=19950126&slug=2101545 accessed 7 May 2017.

"The Gerber Mission Statement" Andrea T. Eliscu, *Ready-set-market!: A Comprehensive Guide to Marketing Your Physician Practice* (Dubuque, IA: Kendall/Hunt Publishing Company, 2002), 100.

"What Is Our Plan?" Peter F. Drucker, *The Five Most Important Questions You Will Ever Ask About Your Organization* (San Francisco, CA: Jossey-Bass Publishers, 1993), v.

"**Healthy-starts in the lives of all children.**" Patricia Jones, Larry Kahaner, *Say It and Live It: The 50 Corporate Mission Statements that Hit the Mark* (New York, NY: Doubleday, a division of Bantam Doubleday Dell Publishing Group, Inc., 1995) 106.

"**Nestle**" Wikipedia https://en.wikipedia.org/wiki/Gerber_ Products_Company accessed 10 May 2017.

"**The first practice is to ask what needs to be done.**" Peter F. Drucker, *Classic Drucker: Essential Wisdom of Peter Drucker from the Pages of Harvard Business Review* (Boston, MA: Harvard Business School Publishing, 2006) 116

"**Effectiveness…is a habit**" Peter F. Drucker, (2009-10-06). *The Effective Executive* (Harperbusiness Essentials) (p. 23). HarperCollins. Kindle Edition.

"**Effectiveness, while capable of being learned, surely cannot be taught.**" Peter F. Drucker, (2009-10-06). *The Effective Executive* (Harperbusiness Essentials). HarperCollins. Kindle Edition.

"**The focus on contribution is the key to effectiveness**" Peter F. Drucker, (2009-10-06). *The Effective Executive* (Harperbusiness Essentials) (p. 52). HarperCollins. Kindle Edition.

CHAPTER 9, VIRTUE

"**Virtue against rage will take up arms and the battle will be short.**" William B. Parsons, *Machiavelli's Gospel: The Critique of Christianity in The Prince* (New York: University of Rochester Press, 2016) 177.

"**Our form of government has no sense unless it is founded in a deeply felt religious faith, and I don't care what it is.**" President Eisenhower archives.gov https://www.eisenhower. archives.gov/all_about_ike/quotes.html accessed 6 May, 2017.

"When hiring key employees, there are only two qualities to look for, judgment and taste." John Baldoni, *Lead Your Boss: The Subtle Art of Managing Up* (New York, NY: AMACOM) 177.

"Only a virtuous people are capable of freedom." Bruce H. Yenawine, Michele R. Costello, *Benjamin Franklin and the Invention of Microfinance* (New York, NY: Routledge, an imprint of Taylor & Francis Group) 23.

"The corporation is an entity only in that it is an expression of each of us as individuals." Max De Pree, *Leadership is an Art*, (New York, NY: Currency Book published by Doubleday a division of Random House, Inc., 2004) 70.

"Everyone for themselves mentality." William Safire and Leonard Safire, *Leadership* (New York, NY: Simon and Schuster, 1990), pp. 111-112.

"You almost don't have to manage them." John Keith Edington, *Great Leaders Never Climb Smooth Mountains How To Avoid The 17½ Routes To Ineffective Leadership* (The Old School, Constable Burton, Leyburn, North Yorkshire: Lulu.com 2013) 26.

CHAPTER 10, PERFECTION

"specialized positions in the organization" Thomas S. Bateman, *et. al. Management* (New York, NY: McGraw-HIll/Irwin, 2013) 31.

"Enormous effort and elaborate planning are required to waste this much money." P. J. O'Rourke, *Parliament of Whores: A Lone Humorist Attempts to Explain the Entire U.S. Government* (New York, NY: Grove Press,1992).

"close enough for private sector work" Jim Geraghty, (2014-06-03). *The Weed Agency: A Comic Tale of Federal Bureaucracy Without Limits* (Kindle Location 783). Crown Publishing Group. Kindle Edition.

"What are you doing in here?" Nick Bilton, *Hatching Twitter: A True Story of Money, Power, Friendship, and Betrayal* (New York, NY: Portfolio/Penguin, 2013).

"Cicero excuses himself for having written a long letter…" William Pinnock, *The Harmonicon, Volume 1* (London, Music Warehouse, 1823), 156.

"Good things, when short, are twice as good." James Geary, *Geary's Guide to the World's Great Aphorists* (New York, NY: Bloomsbury USA, distributed by Holtzbrinck, 2007), 45.

"I know it when I see it" Peter Lattman, *The Origins of Justice Stewart's "I Know It When I See It"* 27 September 2007 **https://blogs.wsj.com/law/2007/09/27/the-origins-of-justice-stewarts-i-know-it-when-i-see-it/** accessed 7 May 2017.

CHAPTER 11, IMPERFECTION

"You can fail 70 percent of the time and still be great." From the 2007 movie, *Martian Child* https://en.wikipedia.org/wiki/Martian_Child accessed 7 May 2017.

"Out of the crooked timber of humanity, no straight thing was ever made." Immanuel Kant, Wikiquote https://en.wikiquote.org/wiki/Immanuel_Kant accessed 7 May 2017.

"Nurture his network." Based on the work of John C. Maxwell, *The 360 Degree Leader: Developing Your Influence from Anywhere in the Organization* (Nashville, TN: Nelson Business, a division of Thomas Nelson Publishers, 2005), 4.

"Georgiana had a minor blemish." Nathaniel Hawthorne, *The Birthmark*, 1843, http://www.online-literature.com/poe/125/ accessed 7 May 2017.

CHAPTER 12, BENEFIT

"Why do you want to work here?" Based on "'You've got to find what you love.' Jobs says," Text of Commencement address to Stanford University, June 12, 2005. http://news.stanford. edu/2005/06/14/jobs-061505/ accessed 7 May 2017.

"They'll work for you with blood and sweat and tears." Simon Sinek says in his TED Talk, September 2009 https://www.ted. com/talks/simon_sinek_how_great_leaders_inspire_action accessed 7 May 2017.

"Why do you want to be president?" Chris Whipple, *The Gatekeepers: How the White House Chiefs of Staff Define Every Presidency* (New York, NY: Crown, 2017) 96.

CHAPTER 13, TRUST

"It cuts down transaction costs," Williumrex, "After Reagan," *National Review,* 18 January 2008 http://www.nationalreview. com/article/223411/after-reaganism-williumrex accessed 7 May 2017.

"An executive who makes many decisions is both lazy and ineffectual." Peter F. Drucker, (2009-10-06). *The Effective Executive* (Harperbusiness Essentials) (p. 129). HarperCollins. Kindle Edition.

"...was a micromanager in the extreme..." Nicholas Carlson, *Marissa Mayer and the Fight to Save Yahoo!* (New York: NY, 12 Twelve, 2015), 302.

"within a few days the hostages were released." Inspired by Gary Noesner, *Stalling for Time: My Life as an FBI Hostage Negotiator* (New York, NY: Random House, 2010).

CHAPTER 14, PROCESS

"Coaching *is* management." Dean Smith and Gerald D. Bell with John Kilgo, *The Carolina Way* (New York: NY, The Penguin Press, 2004). Italics in original.

"Oppenheimer took pleasure *in the work itself.*" Ray Monk, *Robert Oppenheimer: A Life Inside the Center* (New York, NY: Doubleday, a division of Random House, 2013). Italics in original

"The risk of a wrong decision is preferable to the terror of indecision." Rabbi Maimonides, Wikiquote https://en.wikiquote.org/wiki/Talk:Maimonides accessed 7 May 2017.

"I shall see." Robert Greene, (2000-09-01). *The 48 Laws of Power* (Kindle Location 1025). Penguin Group US. Kindle Edition.

CHAPTER 15, INDECISION

"When you enter the range of 40 to 70 percent of all available information, think about making your decision." Colin Powell with Tony Koltz, (2012-05-22). *It Worked for Me: In Life and Leadership* (Kindle Location 2035). Harper. Kindle Edition.

"Roosevelt disagreed with Bohr and bade him good day." William Manchester, *The Glory and the Dream: A Narrative History of America 1932 - 1972.* (Boston-Toronto: Little, Brown and Company, 1973).

"speak plainly on their feet" Thomas E. Ricks, *The Generals: American Military Command from World War II to Today* (New York, NY: Penguin Books, 2012), 199.

"the three R's of numbers: Reduce, Round, and Relate" James C. Humes (2009-02-19). *Speak Like Churchill, Stand Like Lincoln: 21 Powerful Secrets of History's Greatest Speakers* (Kindle Locations 834-835). Crown Publishing Group. Kindle Edition.

"In any moment of decision...The worst thing you can do is nothing." edited by Alan D. Kaye, Charles J. Fox, III, Richard D. Urman, *Operating Room Leadership and Management* (New York, NY: Cambridge University Press, 2012), 32.

CHAPTER 16, PROMOTION

"There are only two things we *can* do." Stanley Weintraub, *A Christmas Far from Home: An Epic Tale of Courage and Survival during the Korean War* (Philadelphia, PA: Da Capo Press, a member of the Perseus Group, 2014), 117. Italics in the original.

"We want mastery." Inspired by Daniel H. Pink, *A Whole New Mind: Why Right-Brainers Will Rule the Future* (New York, NY: Riverhead Books published by the Penguin Group, 2005) 93. Also see video, *Autonomy, Mastery & Purpose* https://www.youtube.com/watch?v=wdzHgN7_Hs8 accessed 8 May 2017.

"Kahn Academy" https://www.khanacademy.org/ accessed 8 May, 2017.

"Biosphere" John Allen, *Me and The Biospheres: A Memoir by the Inventor of Biosphere 2* (Sante Fe, NM: Synergetic Press, 2009).

"cockroaches were fruitful" *10 Lessons from Biosphere 2*, David L. Chandler, *Wired Magazine*, 1 December 2004 https://www.wired.com/2004/12/biosphere/ accessed 8 May, 2017.

"Marilyn Monroe's fashion designer." Mike Hulme, *Can Science Fix Climate Change?: A Case Against Climate Engineering* (Malden, MA: Polity Press, 2014), 91.

"sick trees" Mick Ukleja, Robert L. Lorber, *Who Are You? What Do You Want?: Four Questions That Will Change Your Life* (New York, NY: Perigee Book published by Penguin Group, 2009), 76.

"counterpressure, enliven the soul" Mark Helprin, (2005-07-07). *Freddy and Fredericka* (p. 500). Penguin Group US. Kindle Edition.

"the man who had done so little" Thomas E. Ricks, *The Generals: American Military Command from World War II to Today* (New York, NY: Penguin Books, 2012), 213.

"relaxed" rather than "lazy" Richard Koch, *The 80/20 Principle: The Secret to Achieving More with Less* (New York, NY: Crown Business, 1999).

CHAPTER 17, NARRATIVE

"You were the answer to the General's prayer." Frank Capra, *The Name Above The Title: An Autobiography* (New York, NY: Da Capo Press, a member of the Perseus Books Group, 1971), 322.

"Humans are not ideally set up to understand logic." Daniel H. Pink, *A Whole New Mind: Why Right-Brainers Will Rule the Future* (New York, NY: Riverhead Books published by the Penguin Group, 2005), 102.

"Stories are data with a soul." Dr. Brene Brown, *The power of vulnerability* TED talk https://www.ted.com/talks/brene_brown_on_vulnerability?language=en accessed 8 May, 2017.

"America is a happy-ending nation." William Manchester, *The Glory and the Dream: A Narrative History of America 1932 - 1972.* (Boston-Toronto: Little, Brown and Company, 1973).

"Good teaching is one-fourth preparation and three-fourths theater." Larry Chang, editor, *Wisdom for the Soul: Five Millennia of Prescriptions for Spiritual Healing* (Washington, DC: Gnosophia Publishers, 2006), 700.

"on top of events, and in control" Michael Novak, *The Experience of Nothingness* (New York, NY: Harper & Row, 1970), 114.

CHAPTER 18, ALLIANCES

"**Management's most important power is the veto power.**"
Peter F. Drucker, (2009-10-13). *Management* (Harper & Row
Management Library) (p. 797). HarperCollins. Kindle Edition.

"**and vetoes down**" Peter F. Drucker, (2009-10-13). *Management*
(Harper & Row Management Library) (p. 797). HarperCollins.
Kindle Edition.

"**You should always go to other people's funerals; otherwise,
they won't come to yours.**" http://www.nydailynews.
com/sports/baseball/yankees/yogi-berra-famous-quotes-
legendary-wisdom-article-1.2370926 accessed 8 May, 2017

"**A manager is an *assistant* to his men.**" Julia Vitullo-Martin,
J. Robert Moskin, editors, *The Executive's Book of Quotations*
(New York, NY: Oxford University Press, 1994), 176. Italics
in original.

"**But no more than six stakeholders.**" Erik Larson, "A Checklist
for Making Faster, Better Decisions" in *Harvard Business Review*
https://hbr.org/2016/03/a-checklist-for-making-faster-
better-decisions accessed 8 May, 2017.

"**Leadership is many things.**" Thomas J. Peters and Robert H.
Waterman, Jr., *In Search of Excellence : Lessons from America's
Best-Run Companies* (New York, NY: HarperCollins Publishers,
1982).

"**to reconcile conflicting forces**" Chester Irving Barnard, *The
Functions of the Executive* (Cambridge, MA: Harvard University
Press, 1938), 21.

"**reconcile, not resolve**" Henry Mintzberg, *Managing* (San
Francisco, CA: Berrett-Koehler, Inc., 2009), 158.

"**Three yards and a cloud of dust…**" William V. Levy, *Three yards
and a cloud of dust: The Ohio State football story* (World Publisher
Co., 1966).

"grapevine can be traced to Civil War days" Allan J. Kimmel, *Rumors and Rumor Control: A Manager's Guide to Understanding and Combatting Rumors* (New York, NY: Routledge, Taylor & Francis Group, 2012).

"smells risks and threats early" Colin Powell with Tony Koltz, (2012-05-22). *It Worked for Me: In Life and Leadership* (Kindle Location 1388). Harper. Kindle Edition.

CHAPTER 19, DEBATE

"No man functions at his best without opposition." Colleen McCullough, *Caesar, A Novel* (New York, NY: Avon Books, an imprint of HarperCollins Publishers, 1997).

"give me the benefit of your thinking" Leonard Mosley, *Marshall, Organizer of Victory*, (London, UK: Methuen Publishing, 1982), 366.

"Be able to resign." Donald Rumsfeld, (2013-05-14). *Rumsfeld's Rules: Leadership Lessons in Business, Politics, War, and Life* (Kindle Location 4004). HarperCollins. Kindle Edition.

"lapse in moral courage" Thomas E. Ricks, *The Generals: American Military Command from World War II to Today* (New York, NY: Penguin Books, 2012) 156.

"The machine controls our destiny." Richard Nixon, *Leaders: Profiles and Reminiscences of Men Who Have Shaped the Modern World* (New York, NY: Simon & Schuster, 1984).

"beyond the first encounter" Tiha von Ghyczy, Bolko von Oetinger, Christopher Bassford, editors, *Clausewitz on Strategy: Inspiration and Insight from a Master Strategist* (New York, NY: John Wiley & Sons, 2001), 55.

"Then they don't have a plan anymore." Dan Balz, *Collision 2012: The Future of Election Politics in a Divided America* (New York, NY: Penguin Books, 2013).

"clear triumph of both American technology and managerial methods" Andrea Gabor, *The Capitalist Philosophers: The Geniuses of Modern Business--Their Lives, Times, and Ideas* (New York, NY: Three Rivers Press, member of the Crown Publishing Group, 2000), 138.

"a knock-down-drag-out debate" Robert S. McNamara, Brian VanDeMark, *In Retrospect: The Tragedy and Lessons of Vietnam* (New York, NY: Random House, 1995), 203.

"business research staff" Peter F. Drucker, (2009-10-13). *Management* (Harper & Row Management Library) (p. 763). HarperCollins. Kindle Edition.

"He might see something you don't." David Gergen, *Eyewitness To Power: The Essence of Leadership Nixon to Clinton* (New York, NY: Touchstone, Simon & Schuster, 2000), 184.

"evaluation instrument" Wikipedia https://en.wikipedia.org/wiki/360-degree_feedback accessed 8 May 2015.

"The only inexcusable offense in a commanding officer is to be surprised." Michael Wright, *The Coaches' Chalkboard: Inspiring Quotations for Athletes, Coaches, and Parents* (Lincoln, NE: Writers Club Press, an imprint of iUniverse, Inc., 2002), 14.

"Beware of a surprise..." William Hogeland, *Autumn of the Black* (New York, NY: Farrar, Straus and Giroux, 2017), 13.

"'candor' and 'candle.'" Eric Partridge, *Origins: A Short Etymological Dictionary of Modern English* (Oxon, Great Britain: Routledge an imprint of Taylor & Francis Group, 1958), 74.

"quizzing his staff to get information" Thomas P. O'Neill with William Novak, *Man of the House: The Life and Political Memoirs of Speaker Tip O'Neill* (New York, NY: Random House, 1987), 132.

"How am I doing?" Chris Boyette, "Eulogists remember Ed Koch, New York City's 'quintessential mayor'" CNN.com http://www.cnn.com/2013/02/04/us/ed-koch-funeral/ accessed 9 May, 2017.

"Getting Things Done" is inspired by David Allen in *Getting Things Done: The Art of Stress-Free Productivity* (New York, NY: Penguin Group, 2001).

"Exploding Pintos" Andrea Gabor, *The Capitalist Philosophers: The Geniuses of Modern Business--Their Lives, Times, and Ideas* (New York, NY: Three Rivers Press, member of the Crown Publishing Group, 2000), 140.

"merchants of death" Peter F. Drucker, (2009-10-13). *Management* (Harper & Row Management Library) (p. 329). HarperCollins. Kindle Edition.

"never authorized the change" Robert Lacy, *Ford: The Men and the Machine* (Boston, MA: Little, Brown and Company, 986), 581.

"It just didn't pay to redesign the Pinto." Joan Magretta, *What Management Is: How It Works and Why It's Everyone's Business* (New York, NY: Free Press, a division of Simon & Schuster, 2002).

CHAPTER 20, EXECUTE

"he fights" https://www.whitehouse.gov/1600/presidents/ulys sessgrant accessed 8 May 2017.

"responsible for doing just one thing" Peter Thiel and Blake Masters, (2014-09-16). *Zero to One: Notes on Startups, or How to Build the Future* (p. 123). Crown Publishing Group. Kindle Edition.

"a single tactical action" The US Army, *Commander And Staff Office Guide*, Army Tactics, Techniques, and Procedures, Number 5-0-1, Headquarters, Department of the Army, Washington, DC, (Books Express Publishing: 2011), 2-3.

"ability to consistently Execute" Jack Welch, "GE 2000 Annual Report" http://www.ge.com/annual00/values/ accessed 8 May 2017.

"energy in the one who executes" *The Federalist Papers,* Number 70. http://avalon.law.yale.edu/18th_century/fed70.asp accessed 8 May 2017.

"Gordon Richard Thoman at Xerox" Larry Bossidy, Ram Charan, and Charles Burck, *Execution: The Discipline of Getting Things Done* (New York: NY, Crown Publication, 2003).

"'BuRox' short for 'Bureaucracy-Xerox.'" *Ibid.*

"occasional naked use of power" Thomas J. Peters and Robert H. Waterman, Jr., *In Search of Excellence : Lessons from America's Best-Run Companies* (New York, NY: HarperCollins Publishers, 1982).

CHAPTER 21, DEADLINES

"Excellence, then, is not a choice but a habit." http://blogs.umb.edu/quoteunquote/2012/05/08/its-a-much-more-effective-quotation-to-attribute-it-to-aristotle-rather-than-to-will-durant/ accessed 8 May 2017.

"that there is nothing left to do" Henry Mintzberg, (2013-09-02). *Simply Managing: What Managers Do — and Can Do Better* (Kindle Location 253). Berrett-Koehler Publishers. Kindle Edition.

"cues, routines and rewards" Charles Duhigg, *The Power of Habit: Why We Do What We Do in Life and Business.* (New York, NY: Random House, 2012).

"Reminder, Routine and Reward" James Clear http://jamesclear.com/three-steps-habit-change accessed 8 May 9, 2017

"**Fasting can serve as an automatic reminder to pray**" Steve Chapman *A Look at Life from a Deer Stand Study Guide: Hunting for the Meaning of Life from a Deerstand* (Eugene, OR, Harvest House Publishing, 2012), 20.

"**announce their retirement**" Josh Rottenberg, "5 Brilliant Business Lessons from Motley Crue" fastcompany.com, May 28, 2014 https://www.fastcompany.com/3031014/5-brilliant-business-lessons-from-moetley-cruee-seriously accessed 8 May, 2017.

"**fewer live sacrifices**" Lorin Woolfe, *The Bible on Leadership: From Moses to Matthew -- Management Lessons for Contemporary Leaders* (New York: NY, AMACOM, 2002), 39.

"**Impossible time frames**" Richard Koch, *The 80/20 Principle: The Secret to Achieving More with Less* (New York, NY: Crown Business, 1999).

"**by bellows and meat ax**" Peter F. Drucker, *The Practice of Management* (New Delhi, India: Allied Publishers Pvt. Limited, 1955), 85.

"**staff the opportunities**" Peter F. Drucker, *Management Challenges for the 21st Century* (Burlington, MA: Butterworth-Heinemann, an imprint of Elsevier, 2009), 71.

CHAPTER 22, SALES

"**Find the pain**" David H. Sandler, John Hayes, *You Can't Teach a Kid to Ride a Bike at a Seminar : The Sandler Sales Institute's 7-Step System for Successful Selling* (Beverly Hills, CA: Pegasus Media World, 4ᵗʰ Edition, 1996).

"**it must attract attention**" Wikipedia https://en.wikipedia.org/wiki/AIDA_(marketing) accessed 8 May, 2017.

"**AIDA**" *ibid.*

"Doubts can be paralyzing." David Casstevens, Gary Mack, *Mind gym: an athlete's guide to inner excellence* (New York, NY: 2002), 165.

"Consumers are too good at sniffing out inconsistencies." Seth Godin, *All Marketers are Liars: The Power of Telling Authentic Stories In A Low-Trust World* (New York, NY: Penguin Group, 2009).

"No one was ever fired for buying IBM." Ben Kepes, *Forbes*, 26 January 2105 https://www.forbes.com/sites/benkepes/2015/01/26/as-ibm-readies-to-perform-the-biggest-corporate-employee-cull-in-history-it-claims-cloud-leadership/#5a2ec4453c63 accessed 8 May 2017.

"Anticipate the future." Thomas S. Bateman, *et. al. Management* (New York, NY: McGraw-HIll/Irwin, 2013).

"physically being together" Nicholas Carlson, *Marissa Mayer and the Fight to Save Yahoo!* (New York, NY: Hachette Book Group, 2016).

CHAPTER 23, COMMUNICATION

"There are three roles that all managers perform." Thomas S. Bateman, *et. al. Management* (New York, NY: McGraw-HIll/Irwin, 2013).

"simply communicating" Henry Mintzberg, *Managing* (San Francisco, CA: Berrett-Koehler, Inc., 2009), 28.

"a telephone on his desk" William Manchester, *The Glory and the Dream: A Narrative History of America 1932 - 1972.* (Boston-Toronto: Little, Brown and Company, 1973).

"first executive function" Henry Mintzberg, *Managing* (San Francisco, CA: Berrett-Koehler, Inc., 2009), 28.

"between 60 and 90 percent oral" *Ibid*, 26.

"lost his voice" William Manchester, *The Glory and the Dream: A Narrative History of America 1932 - 1972* (Boston-Toronto: Little, Brown and Company, 1973).

"communicate your message" Jack Welch, LinkedIn https://www.linkedin.com/pulse/20140107141641-86541065-10-resolutions-to-make-it-a-very-good-year accessed 8 May, 2017

"bottomless supply of verbal energy" Lorin Woolfe, *The Bible on Leadership: From Moses to Matthew -- Management Lessons for Contemporary Leaders* (New York: NY, AMACOM, 2002), 100.

"I stand in pause where I shall first begin." William Shakespeare, Hamlet, Act III, Scene 3, lines # 39-61.

"Strategic Silence" James C. Humes, (2009-02-19). *Speak Like Churchill, Stand Like Lincoln: 21 Powerful Secrets of History's Greatest Speakers* (Kindle Location 143). Crown Publishing Group. Kindle Edition.

"He simply gazed across the room." Leonard Mosley, *Marshall, Organizer of Victory*, (London, UK: Methuen Publishing, 1982), 370.

"The Bible is no mere book." Harry E. Richards, *A Guide to Bible Study: A Systematic Course of Graded Lessons for Sunday Schools*, Volume 1, Parts 1-3 (Bloomfield, NJ: Index Publishing Company, 1914), ix.

CHAPTER 24, INERTIA

"Don't take nobody nobody brought." Thomas P. O'Neill with William Novak, *Man of the House: The Life and Political Memoirs of Speaker Tip O'Neill* (New York, NY: Random House, 1987).

"We accumulate victories." Personal conversation with Troy Newman who runs a non-profit, May, 2015.

"Laugh, and the world laughs with you; weep, and you weep alone." Ella Wheeler Wilcox, Wikipedia https://en.wikipedia.org/wiki/Ella_Wheeler_Wilcox accessed 8 May, 2017.

"It is not ideas or opinions which decide, but deeds." Eric Metaxas, *Bonhoeffer: Pastor, Martyr, Prophet, Spy* (Nashville, TN: Thomas Nelson, 2010).

"symptom of victory" Arthur C. Brooks, *The Road to Freedom: How to Win the Fight for Free Enterprise* (New York, NY: Basic Books, a member of the Perseus Books Group, 2012), 27.

"skilled at creating, acquiring, and transferring knowledge" Thomas S. Bateman, *et. al.*, *Management* (New York, NY: McGraw-HIll/Irwin, 2013).

"continuous learning" This is the growth mindset Carol S. Dweck, Ph.D. explains in her book, *Mindset: The New Psychology of Success, How We Can Learn To Fulfill Our Potential Parenting, Business, School, Relationships* (New York, NY: Ballentine Books an imprint of The Random House Publishing Group), 8.

"Engagement means involving individuals in the decisions." W. Chan Kim, Renee Mauborgne, *Blue Ocean Strategy, Expanded Edition: How to Create Uncontested Market Space and Make the Competition Irrelevant* (Boston, MA: Harvard Business Review Press, 2015), 139.

CHAPTER 25, U-NO-DIR

"There are two kinds of football players." Bob Nelson and Peter Economy, *Managing for Dummies* (Hoboken, NJ: Wiley Publishers, 2003).

"If the Boss wants it real bad" inspired by William Oncken, Jr., *Managing Management Time* (New York: Prentice Hall, 1984).

"**U-nO-Dir**" David L. Marquet has more in, "I intend to...", read *Turn the Ship Around!: A True Story of Turning Followers into Leaders* (New York: Portfolio/Penguin, 2013).

CHAPTER 26, VALUE

Bill Whittle didn't invent **Eject! Eject! Eject!**; but he did have a blog by the same name in the early 2000's. He is the inspiration for this passage. https://www.billwhittle.com/content/about-bill accessed 10 May 2017.

"**Discipline of practice**" Jascha Heifetz, "Stopped on the streets of Manhattan and asked how to get to Carnegie Hall, Heifetz is reported to have replied: "Practice, practice, practice."" http://jaschaheifetz.com/about/quotations/ accessed 10 May 2017

As Jack Welch would say, "Don't be a victim." Jack Welch,; Suzy Welch (2009-10-13). *Winning: The Ultimate Business How-To Book* (Kindle Location 164). HarperCollins. Kindle Edition. See also: to *Vanity Fair* in answer to "What words do you most overuse?" "**Don't be a victim.**"

http://www.vanityfair.com/news/2005/05/proust_welch200505 accessed 10 May 2107

"'**support' and 'core**'" Andrea Gabor, *The Capitalist Philosophers: The Geniuses of Modern Business--Their Lives, Times, and Ideas* (New York, NY: Three Rivers Press, member of the Crown Publishing Group, 2000), 322.

"**vital few rather than the trivial many**" Richard Koch, *The 80/20 Principle: The Secret to Achieving More with Less* (New York, NY: Crown Business, 1999), 127.

CHAPTER 27, CREDIT

"There is no limit to what a man can do or where he can go if he doesn't mind who gets the credit." President Reagan had a plaque with the quote sitting on his desk in the Oval Office.

https://www.reaganfoundation.org/ronald-reagan/the-presidency/reagan-the-man/ accessed 7 May 2017. Reagan did not say this in his 1st Inaugural address.

http://www.presidency.ucsb.edu/ws/?pid=43130 accessed 9 May 2017. Video

https://www.youtube.com/watch?v=hpPt7xGx4Xo accessed 9 May 2017.

"Thank the passer" Dean Smith, Gerald D. Bell, and John Kilgo. *The Carolina Way: Leadership Lessons from a Life in Coaching* (New York, NY: Penguin, 2004), 164-5.

"allowing them to patronize him" Gordon S. Wood, *The Americanization of Benjamin Franklin* (New York, NY: Penguin Group, 2004), 59.

"made him his friend by borrowing a book from him" *ibid.*

"Never let him feel he is dependent on you." Leonard Mosley, *Marshall, Organizer of Victory*, (London, UK: Methuen Publishing, 1982).

"Don't keep a careful tally." Morton Blackwell https://www.leadershipinstitute.org/writings/?ID=30 accessed 7 May, 2017.

CHAPTER 28, LOYAL

"tell people who had served loyally that they would have to leave" Donald Rumsfeld, (2013-05-14). *Rumsfeld's Rules: Leadership Lessons in Business, Politics, War, and Life* (Kindle Location 645). HarperCollins. Kindle Edition.

"build your own team— and do it fast" Donald Rumsfeld, (2013-05-14) *Rumsfeld's Rules: Leadership Lessons in Business, Politics, War, and Life* (Kindle Location 650). HarperCollins. Kindle Edition.

"Don't fully trust anyone" Morton Blackwell, Leadership Institute https://www.leadershipinstitute.org/writings/?ID=30 accessed 7 May 9, 2017.

"I don't need you when I'm right." Huey Long, Barry Popik, 29 December 2010 www.barrypopik.com/index.php/new_york_city/entry/i_dont_need_you_when_im_right accessed 7 May 2017.

"go back on either and you're dead" Morton Blackwell, Leadership Institute https://www.leadershipinstitute.org/writings/?ID=30 accessed 7 May, 2017.

"hygiene factors" Frederick Herzberg, Bernard Mausner, Barbara B. Snyderman, *The Motivation to Work* (2nd ed.). (New York, NY: John Wiley, 1959).

"hygiene factors" Frederick Herzberg, (January–February 1968). "One More Time: How Do You Motivate Employees?" *Harvard Business Review.* 46 (1): 53–62.

"pay the rent" Morton Blackwell, Leadership Institute https://www.leadershipinstitute.org/writings/?ID=30 accessed 7 May, 2017.

"Buy a dog!" Max Cryer, *Every Dog Has Its Day: A Thousand Things You Didn't Know about Man's Best Friend.* (Wollombi: Exisle, 2013), 72.

ABOUT THE AUTHOR

JOHN "JACK" WESLEY YOEST, JR., is a Clinical Assistant Professor of Management at The Catholic University of America where he teaches graduate and undergraduate business students. Jack is a senior business mentor in high-technology, medicine, and non-profit and new media consulting. His international expertise is in management training and development, operations, sales, and marketing.

Jack is a columnist for *Small Business Trends* and *The Stream* and has been published by Scripps-Howard, *National Review, The Business Monthly,* and other outlets. He has worked in a number of medical device start-up companies.

Jack has served in government as Assistant Secretary for Health and Human Resources in the Commonwealth of Virginia. He was COO of a $5-billion budget and acted as the CTO for the Secretary of Health and Human Resources where he was responsible for the successful Y2K conversion for the 16,000-employee unit.

Jack is a former Captain in the US Army. He earned an MBA from George Mason University and completed graduate work in the International Operations Management Program at Oxford University. He has been active on a number of boards and has run several marathons.

Jack and his wife Charmaine live in the Washington, D.C., area with their five children.